PRAISE F
HARRY HO

★ "Together with its companion, stimulating portraits of
two colorful, driven historical figures."

—*Kirkus Reviews*, starred review

"This informative biography is a chatty and engaging
read for the unitiated as well as for those who thought
they knew everything about one of the greatest
magicians of all time."

—*Booklist*

"A lighthearted and easy look at some of the world's
most famous celebrities ... The illustrations may prove
to be comforting to fiction readers who enjoy diary style
series like Jeff Kinney's Diary of a Wimpy Kid."

—*School Library Journal*

HARRY
Houdini

Kjartan Poskitt
Illustrations by Geraint Ford

Abrams Books for Young Readers

NEW YORK

All the facts in *First Names: Harry Houdini* have been carefully checked and are accurate to the best of our knowledge. Many of the stories rely on people's memories and newspaper reports, and sometimes it's impossible to separate the truth from the legend, but we have brought Harry back to life as faithfully as we can.

Library of Congress Control Number 2018966474

Paperback ISBN 978-1-4197-4090-9

Text copyright © 2019 Kjartan Poskitt
Illustrations copyright © 2019 Geraint Ford
Book design by Max Temescu and Jade Rector

2019 © as UK edition. First published in 2019
by David Fickling Books Limited

Published in paperback in 2020 by Abrams Books for Young Readers, an imprint of ABRAMS. Originally published in hardcover by Abrams Books for Young Readers in 2019. All rights reserved. No portion of this book may be reproduced, stored in a retrieval system, or transmitted in any form or by any means, mechanical, electronic, photocopying, recording, or otherwise, without written permission from the publisher.

Printed and bound in U.S.A.
10 9 8 7 6 5 4 3 2 1

Abrams Books for Young Readers are available at special discounts when purchased in quantity for premiums and promotions as well as fundraising or educational use. Special editions can also be created to specification. For details, contact specialsales@abramsbooks.com or the address below.

Abrams® is a registered trademark of Harry N. Abrams, Inc.

ABRAMS The Art of Books
195 Broadway, New York, NY 10007
abramsbooks.com

Contents

INTRODUCTION

July 7, 1912, New York, New York

Harry stood on a barge on New York's East River. Over on the quayside, a massive crowd had gathered to watch what he was about to do.

Anybody might have thought Harry was going for a swim, but then one of his assistants clamped his wrists in a pair of handcuffs.

"Hey, Mr. Houdini, are those your own cuffs?" asked one reporter.

"Yeah, I bet they've got a secret catch to release them!" said another.

Harry gave them a cold stare. "Police cuffs," he said in his German accent. Then he shoved his hands toward the reporters. "You want to try them?"

The handcuffs were locked tight and looked heavy. The reporter shook his head!

Harry flashed a cheeky smile, then stepped back. He had a set of leg irons locked around his ankles.

Harry stared into the water. Surely he wasn't going in? The weight of all that metal would drag him straight to the bottom! And just in case that wasn't bad enough, three strong men then lifted him into a wooden box and **nailed the lid down**.

What on earth was Harry going to do?

The barge crane hoisted the box up above the deck, then swung it out over the river. The crowd on the quayside had been getting louder, first gasping then groaning . . . but **suddenly they fell silent**.

For a moment the box hung in space, then the crane started letting the rope out. The box hit the surface of the water then sunk down. A few last bubbles of air came up as it disappeared deep into the darkness.

Screams came from the crowd on the quayside. People at the back pushed forward, trying to see what was happening, and the ones at the front struggled not to fall over the edge!

All around the barge, reporters were scribbling away madly. Why didn't the men working the ropes pull the box back up? In fact, they were just letting more and more rope out! **Didn't they know Harry was down there**?

A whole minute passed, but then the crowd began to cheer. People pointed to a spot further down the river. There was something splashing about in the water. It was man and he was waving.

It was Harry! **He'd escaped from the box!**

Thank goodness he was safe, because there was no doubt about it—Harry could easily have died!

What do you mean? I never left anything to chance. I had too much to lose.

Like money and fame?

No, no, I mean my wife, Bess, and my mother too. And I had so many other things I wanted to do.

Such as?

See the world, make films, fly airplanes. I even tried to contact the spirits of dead people. Believe me, I had no intention of drowning in that box.

So, it *wasn't* dangerous?

Of course it was dangerous! Would you want to try it?

No way! But why did you do it, Harry?

Because I was the greatest showman who ever lived, so the sooner you stop with the questions and start telling my story, the better!

1   WHO WAS HARRY?

If you wanted to describe Harry in one word, HUNGRY would be a good one. When he was growing up, he was often hungry for food, but more importantly he was always **hungry for adventure, challenges, fame, and success**. He refused to let anything or anyone beat him.

Harry always said he was American, but this wasn't true. He was actually born in the city of Budapest on March 24, 1874 . . . and Budapest is the capital of Hungary. So you could say **he was a hungry Hungarian**.

And his real name wasn't even Harry, it was Ehrich!

Shhh, Mother! Don't tell everybody!

(Harry and his mom didn't speak in English; they always spoke to each other in German.)

HOW DID HARRY END UP IN AMERICA?

Harry's dad was Mayer Samuel Weisz. He was an important Jewish scholar and lawyer, so he was known as Rabbi Weisz.

Harry's mom was a small lively woman, twelve years younger than the rabbi and named Cecilia. When Harry was a baby, he already had older brothers plus a stepbrother from his dad's first marriage.

At first, life was good, but when Harry was just one year old, **his father suddenly ran off**!

Nobody knows for sure why he went, but according to one story, Rabbi Weisz had been **challenged to a duel** by a Hungarian prince, and had ended up killing him!

It was three years before the rabbi could arrange for his family to join him. In the meantime Cecilia struggled to raise the boys on her own, and that included baby Theodore who was born after his father had gone. Little Harry was just starting to walk and talk; he could see how hard his mom had to work to look after them all, and **he adored her** for it. Whenever he screamed she would hug him and he would calm down so quickly it was almost like magic.

Of course she hugged the other boys too, but they soon grew out of it. Harry never did—even as a grown-up!

Harry's dad sent letters home from the United States, and eventually, when Harry was four, the family sailed across the ocean to join him. They all crammed into the cheapest section of the steamship *Frisia*, sleeping on wooden benches and eating disgusting food. Harry and baby Theodore clung on to their mom for thirteen long days and nights as the boat rumbled and rocked its way to America.

When they arrived, it must have seemed like an alien world. The language was strange, the buildings were all modern, and everything was faster and louder. Even their name changed, because as soon as they got off the boat the officials decided the "z" in Weisz looked too foreign and so it became Weiss. They finally settled down with their father in the state of Wisconsin by the Great Lakes, in a place called Appleton.

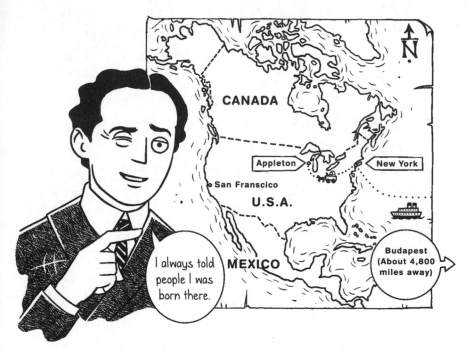

And in some ways, it *was* where Harry was born, because Appleton was where **little Ehrich started to turn into Harry Houdini**.

2   HARRY AND THE HEADLESS MAN

By the time Harry was eight years old, he had five brothers and a baby sister and life hadn't gotten any easier. Harry's mom never managed to learn English, so the family all spoke in German. (Harry never lost his German accent!) Harry's dad struggled to find work, and on one awful day, Harry's baby sister, Carrie Gladys, had **an accident that left her almost blind**.

Money was so short that Harry didn't go to school much. Instead he did anything he could to bring home a few extra coins. He ran errands, polished shoes, sold newspapers, and he even begged on the streets.

Sometimes he'd be joined by his little brother Theodore, whose family nickname had become "Deshi" for short and then "Dash." Harry and Dash were best friends for life. One afternoon they turned a disaster into an adventure, when they proudly headed home with $2 in change. Dash had insisted on carrying it.

I hope you've got that money safe.

Oh no!

When they got home, all that was left was one tiny nickel. Cecilia was almost in tears. Harry couldn't bear it, so he grabbed Dash and ran to a florist's, where they bought a single flower and sold it to a stranger for a dime.

They went back in to buy two more flowers, sold those, and went back again until they had enough money to replace the $2 they had lost!

Harry was always desperate to cheer his mom up and help her forget how hard their life was. Sometimes, if he had money to hand over, he hid the coins in his clothes and hair and **made them appear by "magic."** The magic wasn't terribly clever. He might just ask his mom to shake him so the coins fell out, which made her laugh. Harry was discovering what it was like to entertain an audience and he loved it.

The Red Stockings

By the time he was nine, Harry had started putting on a completely different sort of show for the family and their neighbors.

Behold! I am Ehrich, Prince of the Air!

Are those my red woollen stockings?

Harry was very athletic, and wanted to find out what he could make his body do. He was always fascinated by the circus acrobats who came to town, and so **he taught himself to walk a tightrope**. He had also seen a contortionist who could bend his body in strange ways and fit himself into a tiny box, so Harry tried that too! He even invented his own tricks, such as bending over backwards and picking up pins with his teeth. (And he claimed he could do the same trick with his eyelids!)

He spent so much time with the circus people that eventually they let him appear in a show and even paid him 35 cents, his first ever showbiz wages! It was enough to buy a bag of groceries and put a smile on his mom's face.

For hours every day, Harry would exercise and stretch and twist himself until his whole body became very strong and very bendy. He was actually dreaming of becoming a sportsman—a runner or a swimmer—but **all this training would be vital** for his escapes later on!

MAGIC FINGERS

Harry never let himself rest. Above all, he kept his hands busy. He found books in the library which taught him little bits of magic involving coins and cards. Harry would study these books through the night, practicing the tricks over and over again. Even at mealtimes **he'd eat with one hand and be twiddling a coin with the other**, and soon he was performing on street corners to earn tips from passersby.

To do these tricks well, you have to have perfect control of every single finger. Give it a try! First, run through these finger patterns keeping your open fingers straight!

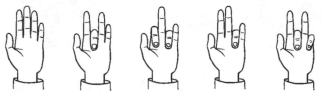

You can make cards or coins appear and disappear in your hand! Here's how Harry did it:

Coin in hand. Cover it up. Now it's gone! Cover it up again. It's back!

The Secret

 Hold the coin between your first and little fingers. Cover your hand, then flip the middle fingers under.

It looks like the coin has gone, but it's actually hidden behind your middle fingers.

 Put your middle fingers back and the coin reappears! With lots of practice you can do this quickly!

It takes a long time to get it right. No wonder Harry practiced so much!

Harry's Strange Hobby

When his body was too tired to exercise anymore, Harry's brain was still busy. He started to fiddle with the locks on the cupboards at home. He saw them as puzzles—could he undo them without using a key?

Most locks have a set of little levers inside them which stop the bolt moving so the door stays shut. When the key turns, it lifts the levers out of the way so that the bolt can slide across and then the door will open. The levers have to be lifted exactly the right amount, which is easy with the key, but Harry worked out how to lift them with a buttonhook, like this one:

Buttonhook

He couldn't resist using his new skill, and one morning, when Harry was eleven, everybody in the street woke up to find **all their doors had been unlocked**.

Harry's dad was not amused, but his mom made a clever suggestion. Instead of punishing him, Harry was sent to live with a locksmith named Mr. Hanauer. It was perfect for Harry! He'd get up early every morning and go out for a long hard run, then he'd come back and spend the whole day investigating every different kind of lock. Clever locks, heavy locks, tiny locks, trick locks . . . Harry saw how they were put together, how all the little springs and levers moved and, of course, **how to pick them open**! He was such a fast learner that one day he took Mr. Hanauer completely by surprise.

Two sandwiches later . . .

Although he was pleased with his little trick, he never imagined it would ever be of any use to him. Harry knew exactly how he was going to find fame and fortune. He was going to be a runner or a swimmer or even a boxer in the Olympic Games! But that was before his dad took him to a show that **completely blew his mind** . . .

HARRY HAS A NIGHTMARE

The theater was dark and the stage curtains were black. Dr. Lynn stepped out in front of the footlights and introduced himself. He was English and he started his show with small tricks and a stream of jokes, before calmly announcing that he was going to **cut a man to pieces and put him back together**.

Harry didn't quite know what to expect, until a screen was pulled aside. There was a real live man standing upright tied to a board. The man could scratch his head and speak to the audience, so Harry knew it wasn't a dummy! But surely he wouldn't really be chopped up, not in front of all these people?

The magician put the assistant to sleep with a spell, then pulled out a long curved sword and raised it up. A few people in the audience groaned and covered their eyes. Harry couldn't bear to watch, but he couldn't bear to miss it either. He swallowed hard and stared at the tied-up man. The sword came down and **chopped off** the man's arm, which hung there, held by the rope. Dr. Lynn pulled it free and put it to the side of the stage. Amazingly, there was no blood anywhere! He raised the sword again and chopped off the assistant's leg. Once again—no blood!

Finally he threw a black cloth over the assistant's head and waved the sword. The head came away wrapped in the cloth, just leaving an empty space above the neck. Dr. Lynn then carried the black bundle to the front of the stage. "Who wants it?" he shouted. Everybody was trembling and groaning, but then the cloth fell open. It was empty!

The trick ended with a screen being pulled in front of the rest of the body, and then a few moments later the assistant walked out **completely unharmed**.

The relieved audience went wild. Harry jumped to his feet and applauded with them, then looked back at his dad, who gave him a wink and a smile.

It gave me nightmares afterwards. It was great!

That show stuck in Harry's mind forever, and it taught him two important lessons.

The first was that audiences liked to let their imaginations run wild! Harry had been thrilled by the high tightrope walkers at the circus, but Dr. Lynn's trick was even better. It was creepy, it was dangerous, and it put people **on the edge of their seats**, so it was exactly the sort of thing Harry wanted to do!

The second lesson was this: don't let anybody steal your tricks. But he learned that one much later.

The real Dr. Lynn was very famous, but there's no record of him being in Wisconsin at that time. The man Harry saw was almost certainly an imposter, making money by stealing the real doctor's ideas and pretending to be him.

Thank goodness Harry didn't realize this at the time. His deeply religious dad had always taught him that stealing was a sin, so even when Harry was at his poorest, he never stole anything in his life. More importantly, if anyone ever tried to steal from him, **they were asking for trouble**!

SO HOW WAS IT DONE?

The trick relied on one of the most useful tools in magic—black velvet. The stage would have a black velvet curtain at the back, and then if the lighting was right, anything else in front of it covered in black velvet would seem invisible. To make the man's head disappear, the magician would throw the cloth over him, then sneak a black velvet hood over his head. When the cloth was pulled away, the head would look like it had disappeared! More black velvet and dummy parts created the illusion of the arm and leg coming away.

If you cover your whole body in black velvet, it will look like your head's floating!

These days we're used to seeing strange effects on TV, in films, and on the internet; however, back in the 1880s, before everyone had cameras, people only ever saw what was happening in real life in front of them. So when they watched something that seemed impossible, it really freaked them out!

3   HARRY AND THE OTHER HOUDINIS

By the time Harry was fourteen, the family had hit hard times. Rabbi Weiss wasn't getting enough work in Wisconsin, so they moved to New York, hoping for better luck. The city was big, loud, and smelly, and they were so hungry that Harry had to play a clever trick to get himself a real job.

Bloomingdale's on Broadway is a huge store where all the rich people go. Back in the year 1889, this same building was a clothing workshop called:

> ## H. Richter's Sons Neckwear

One day another much smaller sign hung on the door, saying: "Help Wanted." It had attracted a long line of people all hoping for an interview. They had arrived early and done their best to look sharp, but then, as the story goes, a young man appeared, said "excuse me" and went to the front of the line. He took the sign down, then turned to the crowd and announced, "Thank you for coming, but I'm afraid we've already hired someone."

Everybody grumbled and wandered away. Then the young man **stepped inside and introduced himself**.

"Hello," he said to the foreman in his crisp German accent, holding his hand out for a handshake. "I'm Ehrich Weiss. I've come about that job."

Before the foreman could reply, the young man looked over his shoulder at the empty street.

"It looks like no one else is interested," he said. "So I guess I'm hired."

And that's how Harry got his **first real job**.

Harry never wasted a chance. He worked hard and impressed the firm so much that soon he had talked them into giving his brother Dash a job, and their dad was even taken on for a while.

Harry and Dash were both fans of magic, and they spent their free time practicing tricks along with another factory worker named Jacob Hyman. One day Jacob saw a book sticking out of Harry's bag.

"What's this, Ehrie?" asked Jacob. (Harry's friends called him "Ehrie" instead of "Ehrich.")

"It's all about the French magician Robert-Houdin," said Harry. "He died twenty years ago, but he completely changed what magic looked like."

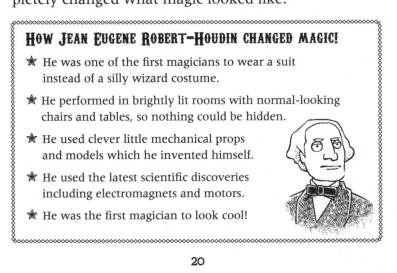

HOW JEAN EUGENE ROBERT-HOUDIN CHANGED MAGIC!

★ He was one of the first magicians to wear a suit instead of a silly wizard costume.

★ He performed in brightly lit rooms with normal-looking chairs and tables, so nothing could be hidden.

★ He used clever little mechanical props and models which he invented himself.

★ He used the latest scientific discoveries including electromagnets and motors.

★ He was the first magician to look cool!

Harry and Jacob were older than Dash and had both managed to save a bit of money, so together they took a chance and left their jobs at the tie factory. They wanted to do something similar to Harry's hero Robert-Houdin, so they formed an act called the Brothers Houdini. And Harry got nicknamed Harry because it sounded like his nickname "Ehrie."

So that's how Ehrich Weiss became Harry Houdini. **Now all he had to do was make himself famous**.

THE METAMORPHOSIS

As well as doing tricks with cards and coins, Harry decided they needed something spectacular. He bought an expensive trick called the Metamorphosis from a retired magician, which was perfect for himself and Jacob to perform together on the streets of New York.

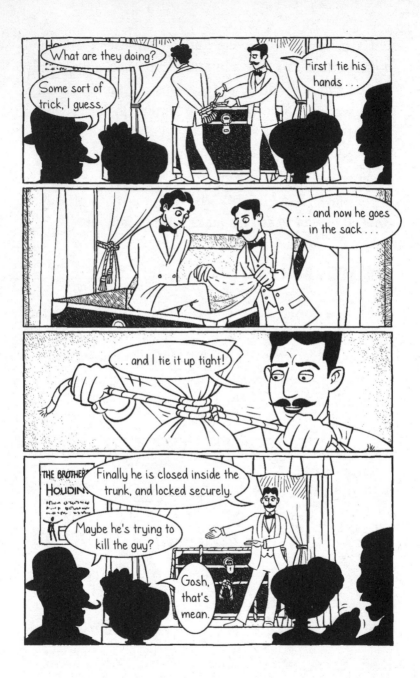

Ropes, Sacks, and Secret Panels

The Metamorphosis was three tricks in one. Here's how a simple version would work.

1. The Tied Hands

When rope is being tied, turn wrists sideways to make it tight.

Turn wrists inward to loosen the rope and slip it off.

2. The Sack Escape

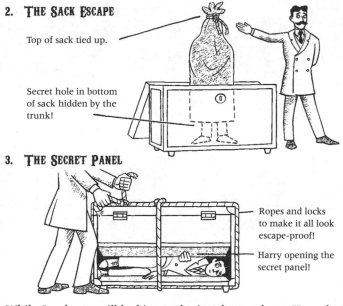

Top of sack tied up.

Secret hole in bottom of sack hidden by the trunk!

3. The Secret Panel

Ropes and locks to make it all look escape-proof!

Harry opening the secret panel!

While Jacob was still locking and tying the trunk up, Harry had already gotten out and was hiding behind it. As soon as Jacob shut the curtain, they would swap places. Then, while Harry was unlocking the trunk lid, Jacob had time to get in the back and into the sack.

The Deathbed Promise

The Metamorphosis was Harry and Jacob's best trick, but they didn't get many bookings. Then, just a year after giving up his job, things got much tougher for Harry. He'd been working across town when a messenger boy ran up to him and said, "Get home, magician, your father's dying."

Harry dashed back to find his father lying in the bed with the rest of the family around him. Although Harry wasn't the eldest, his father had decided Harry was the one he could rely on the most.

Then the old man turned to Cecilia and smiled. "One day Ehrich will fill your apron with gold."

These were the last words Harry's dad spoke, and Harry took them very seriously. Every week, no matter how bad things were, **he made it his duty to give his mother money**. As well as working with Jacob, he started performing on his own anywhere that would have him. That's how he ended up in the Dime Museums.

THE DREADFUL DIME MUSEUMS

Dime Museums—so named because you paid a dime to get in—pretended to be educational. Some museums had waxworks of famous people or perhaps an art gallery showing fakes of famous paintings, but Dime Museums were mostly freak shows.

You might see stuffed monsters made from lots of different animal bits stitched together. There would be peculiar skeletons, shrunken heads, and one museum even showed a brown shrivelled lump and claimed it was "President Abraham Lincoln's Last Poo."

These museums also had shows that ran all day and into the night, with audiences coming and going as they liked. The performers would do a few minutes each, and most of them didn't do much—they were just there to be stared at!

THE GREAT LENTINI

JAKE THE TWO-HEADED CALF

BIG ELLA THE GIANT LADY

Harry often did up to **twenty performances a day** in the Dime Museums. It was hard work. However these shows were really good practice for his tricks, and he picked up some useful skills. He learned all about trick knots and rope escapes from an Australian called George Dexter, and a man who had no arms showed Harry how to undo knots **with his toes**!

THE OTHER BROTHERS HOUDINI

Harry and Jacob kept the Brothers Houdini act going for two years, but finally Jacob refused to do it any more and Harry was left wondering what to do with the Metamorphosis trunk.

It cost me $25, which was all my savings, so I couldn't waste it, but I couldn't do the trick on my own!

The Brothers Houdini were still getting occasional bookings, which Harry couldn't afford to turn down, so he got his brother Dash to help out. Dash was always fun to be with, and they carried on as the Brothers Houdini until 1894, when things took a very different turn.

One evening Harry and Dash were performing in Coney Island—a seaside area on the edge of New York City. In those days it had the **biggest and best funfairs** in the world. The island theaters were full of different acts, including a song-and-dance group called the Floral Sisters. Dash was always chasing girls, and after the show he'd set up a date with one of the Floral Sisters, but two of them turned up.

In fact, nobody can remember the girl that Dash went out with, but the other girl was named Bess and, by the end of the month, **Harry had married her**!

Bess's full name was Wilhelmina Beatrice Rahner, and she had been brought up in New York by her very strict German mother. At sixteen, she'd left home looking for adventure, and two years later she'd only gotten as far as Coney Island. She was cute, mischievous, funny, and ready to take a chance, so Harry and Bess suited each other perfectly.

The only thing that could have stopped Harry from marrying Bess would have been if his mother didn't like her, but Cecilia took to Bess immediately, especially as Bess could chat away to her in German.

Unfortunately, Bess's mom wasn't quite so happy. She was an old-fashioned Roman Catholic and was so upset about her daughter marrying a Jew that she didn't speak to Bess for twelve years!

The other big problem facing them was that Harry had absolutely no money, but Bess didn't let that stop her . . . even though **she had to buy her own wedding ring** and lend Harry two dollars for the marriage licence!

That might not sound like a good start, but for Harry and Bess it was the beginning of an amazing adventure that would last a lifetime.

Harry had loads of exciting plans for the two of them, especially since Bess was very small and agile, so she was perfect to take over as Harry's new magic partner. Dash didn't mind because he had only been helping out as a favor—once he had even ruined the show by **getting stuck** in the trunk!

Harry and Bess were going to call themselves the Houdinis, and together the two of them would travel the world with their show, making good money and having the most wonderful time. But before that happened, Harry asked Bess to join him and Dash on a late-night walk. Just as a clock chimed midnight, they stopped on a bridge. Harry told Bess and Dash to raise their hands and make him a solemn promise.

Bess was really worried until she realized that Harry was showing how much he trusted her. After all, he'd known Dash all his life, but he'd only met her a few weeks before. Dash and Bess were **the only two people that Harry shared all his secrets with**, and the very next day he started to teach Bess everything she needed to know to help with his shows.

Harry was twenty, he finally had the perfect partner, and he was confident that fame and fortune were just around the corner.

But were they?

4   HARRY HITS THE BOTTOM

In those days it was unusual for a man and a woman to perform tricks together, and after a couple of months the Houdinis got a really exciting offer: A week at Tony Pastor's Theater on New York's 14th Street!

Pastor's had always been famous for variety shows, with singers, jugglers, comedians, and magicians. Lots of acts that started there had gone on to great things, so Harry promised Bess **this would be their big break**.

Harry knew he had to make the most of this chance, so he spent all the money they had advertising the show in the local newspapers.

January 7, 1895, New York, New York

At last, the day arrived. The show had about twelve different acts altogether, with the best ones going on at the end. As Harry and Bess were almost unknown, they were one of the first. They were really excited as they stepped onto the stage, but things didn't go quite as they expected.

There were **only twenty-three people** in the audience, and two of those were the cleaners. Most performers would have been tempted to give up and go home, but not Harry . . .

Even if only ONE person buys a ticket, they deserve to get what they paid for. The show MUST go on!

Harry and Bess went out and performed as though they were in front of thousands. When they finished, there were a few polite claps. They smiled and took a big bow, then Bess ran offstage and burst into tears.

Harry was furious, but most of all he felt bad for Bess, especially after he'd built her hopes up. While Harry was clearing their props from the stage, someone else saw how upset Bess was.

Maggie Cline was a loud, jolly singer known as the Irish Queen and she was the big star of the show. She took one look at Bess's sad face, then reached for her makeup bag.

Bess had never had a glamorous makeover before, and when she ran to show Harry, he hardly recognized her. It turned out that Maggie had watched their act, and liked the Houdinis so much that she bullied Tony Pastor into giving them a bigger part in the show.

Without Maggie's little act of kindness Bess might never have coped with the miserable months that were to come.

THE CIRCUS TRAIN

At first things weren't too bad. After their week at Pastor's Theater, Harry and Bess went on tour with the Welsh Brothers Circus. It wasn't the big break Harry had hoped for, but they were paid $20 (about $950 today) a week and the food was great! The Houdinis were sharing the show with clowns, jugglers, strongmen, acrobats, fire-eaters, horses, and lions and they all traveled around the country together **on a big circus train**. In addition to the magic, they had to do whatever else was asked of them. Bess sang and made costumes, and Harry was "Projea, the Wild Man of Mexico." He'd wear thick makeup and rags, then throw himself around inside a cage and even pretend to eat burning cigarettes. Ouch!

Projea, the Wild Man of Mexico

Harry never missed a chance to pick up new skills from other circus performers, like sword-swallowing, fire-eating, and even regurgitating (swallowing objects, then neatly bringing them back up).

Best of all was the East Indian Needle Trick, which Harry learned from an old Hindu man. It looked freaky and dangerous—just the sort of trick that Harry loved best!

1 Harry shows his mouth is empty.

2 Harry lies about 100 needles on his tongue, and then swallows a long piece of cotton.

3 Harry washes it all down with a glass of water.

Eeeek!

4 Ooooh!

ABSOLUTELY DO NOT TRY THIS!

The secret is that Harry already had a set of needles threaded on the cotton and wound up neatly together before the trick started. One hundred needles aren't much bigger than a couple of matchsticks, so when Harry pulled his cheeks apart for people to inspect his mouth, he tucked the needles behind one of his fingers!

When Harry pretended to swallow the loose needles and thread, he just pushed them all against the top of his mouth. (He had to practice very carefully with his tongue!) After he had pulled the threaded needles out, he took another drink of water, and secretly spat the loose needles and thread into the glass. Nobody would see them in the water unless they were extremely close by.

Harry Has a Brainwave

After six months the circus tour ended and Harry and Bess had to look for work wherever they could find it.

All the time they worked on improving the Metamorphosis. One night Harry had a great idea. He realized that having his hands tied together with rope looked too easy, so instead **he used a set of handcuffs** which he could quickly get off and Bess could slip on. The idea worked so well, he started using handcuffs in a new act of his own.

At first it might have seemed like a silly idea. After all, whoever heard of a famous lockpicker? But it did look pretty good on the posters. Harry let the challenger put the cuffs on him, then he would disappear into a little square tent onstage—his "ghost house"— so nobody could see what he was doing.

HOUDINI
WIZARD OF
SHACKLES

Bring your own handcuffs!
$50 reward
paid if he cannot
free himself.

Moments later he would come out waving the cuffs in the air, though occasionally Harry's hands ended up ripped and bloody! Bess was furious that Harry offered a reward when they didn't have any money, but Harry never failed, so he NEVER had to pay the fifty dollars!

HARRY GOES TO PRISON

November 22, 1895, Gloucester, Massachusetts

Harry and Bess found themselves touring with a show that wasn't doing very well—there was a danger none of them would be paid. The company put up posters and performers went around the streets shouting and singing and handing out leaflets. Then Harry had an idea.

He marched into the police station and asked them to put their best handcuffs on him. The police were a bit surprised, but eventually they cuffed him with an old pair. Harry turned his back on everyone, and a few seconds later he tossed the empty cuffs over his shoulder. **The police were amazed**!

Next they got out their best set of new handcuffs and clamped them on Harry's wrists. Moments later— *ping*! Once again, the cuffs were off. The police examined Harry's hands to see if he had strange rubber bones or another way of slipping out of the cuffs but no, **they hadn't a clue how he did it**.

Harry was so pleased, that he went on to challenge the police in every town and city the show visited.

When everybody heard about the man that the police couldn't hold, the show sold out!

They traveled down the East Coast, then up through mid-America, passing through Kansas and Chicago and on into Canada. Harry always made sure the newspapers were there to watch as he was locked in two or three sets of handcuffs at once. The police could shackle his legs too, but **Harry escaped every time**.

Thanks to Harry's clever idea, the show started doing really well . . . until the manager suddenly ran off with all the money. Despite all Harry's skills and publicity stunts, he and Bess were left with nothing.

DOWN AND DESPERATE

Harry and Bess spent two more years traveling around the country, carrying everything they owned packed in the Metamorphosis trunk. Wherever they went Harry wrote letters and postcards home to his mom, and every single week he sent her money, even when they could hardly support themselves. Harry only ever slept for **four hours a night**, and in the early mornings he would slip out and try to haggle cheap food from the market traders. Some nights when they finished late and were setting off early, Harry and Bess would sleep huddled together on train station platforms and often they could only afford a single cup of coffee for breakfast between them.

The Houdinis appeared in some of the cheapest and roughest places, like Huber's Dime Museum in New York. Huber's was on the same street as Tony Pastor's Theater, but it was so different it might as well have been a million miles away. They even performed in beer

halls where the audiences could shout for "the Hook" and a huge hook on a stick would appear from the side and yank the performers off the stage! The audience thought this was hilarious, but it made the acts look really stupid and they hated it. That's why Harry was constantly working on new skills to satisfy his audiences.

Calling himself the King of Cards, he would make handfuls of playing cards appear and disappear in thin air (a bit like the coin trick on page 12, but a LOT harder!). Harry was even an expert at throwing cards! Magicians call this "card scaling."

He'd take a playing card from a pack and throw it so hard that it would stick into a piece of wood. He could even toss a card so that it went around and **came back like a boomerang**. He combined the trick with a somersault he learned from the circus acrobats to produce this three-second wonder:

1. Harry flicks a card over the audience.

2. Harry does a backflip as the card changes direction.

3. Harry then catches the card.

Harry and Bess were really good at what they did, but there were too many other people doing similar things. What the Houdinis needed was **something special** to capture the public's imagination.

HARRY TALKS TO THE DEAD

It was autumn in the year 1897 and Dr. Hill's Medicine Show had come to town! Usually a medicine show was like a traveling Dime Museum. There would be a few acts and curiosities to attract an audience, then a "doctor" would take to the stage and sell his miracle cures, claiming they could heal any illness or infection. But Dr. Hill's show was special because it featured Professor Houdini and Mademoiselle Beatrice Houdini. They were two spirit mediums—who claimed **they could talk to the dead**.

Bess invited two members of the audience to come up and tie Harry to a chair. Next to Harry would be a small table holding some noisy toys such as whistles and a little drum. Bess would pull a screen around Harry and the table and stand back. The lights dimmed and the audience heard Harry call to the "spirits." He'd exaggerate his German accent to make it sound spookier. The whistles tooted, the drum banged, and then the toys started flying out over the top of the screen. Bess pulled the screen aside to show Harry was still tied to the chair, then she put it back again.

A few seconds later Harry stepped out, "freed by the spirits." He then closed his eyes and called out names of people in the audience and passed on messages **from their dead relatives**.

The audience loved it, but of course it was all pretend. Harry could slip ropes on and off as easily as pulling his socks up, so throwing the toys over the screen was simple. As for the messages—in the afternoon before the show, he and Bess listened out for local gossip. They even went down to the cemetery to see if there were any new gravestones showing the names and ages of people who had recently died. Even better, they would talk to the gravediggers, because they always had good stories to tell!

Sometimes Bess went onstage wearing a heavy blindfold and they'd start with a mind reading act. Harry would borrow objects from members of the audience and Bess would be able to describe each one perfectly! Then she'd go into a trance, and have spooky visions. On one famous occasion, there had been a murder in the town and **she described exactly what had happened** and what the murderer was wearing, but then she rather conveniently fainted before she could say his name. There was nearly a riot and the police were called . . . and Dr. Hill's Medicine Show sold out for weeks afterwards!

HOW TO BE A MIND READER!

Harry had read about mind reading in one of Robert-Houdin's books. He could secretly tell Bess whatever she needed to know through an ingenious set of code words and signals. Here's how Dave and Amrita might use a code to do a trick like this on Lucy. Amrita needs to hide where she can't see anything.

Dave has a table with lots of things on it and he asks Lucy to touch one of them. Dave then askes Amrita some questions.

This is a very simple code. If Dave's question starts with the word "is" then Amrita answers, "No." Otherwise she answers, "Yes." Of course Harry and Bess's codes were a lot more complex than that!

Although Harry and Bess did quite well as spirit mediums, they began to hate the act. It had started as a bit of fun, but soon they realized they were making money off of desperate people. What's more, Harry himself wanted to believe in the spirit world, because he would have loved to get a real message from his own dead father. The thought that someone might try to trick him with a pretend message made Harry feel sick. It was cheating—and **Harry hated cheats**!

BESS BACKS OUT

In 1898, Harry and Bess toured with the Welsh Brothers Circus again. They really enjoyed it, but when the tour finished, Bess couldn't bear to go back to the Dime Museums and beer halls. She'd had enough of rough audiences, grubby stages, and rotten pay. **Bess refused to carry on**.

With nowhere else to go, they went to live with Harry's mom in New York. Her house was small and already packed with Harry's younger brothers and sister, but Cecilia would never have turned them away.

Harry set up "Professor Houdini's Magic School," and tried to sell little booklets with all his magic secrets. He even offered to sell his equipment, but nobody was interested. Finally he made a deal with Bess. He would work the Dime Museums and beer halls on his own for one more year to see if his luck changed. If he couldn't make enough money, he'd give up magic and get a real job with regular wages.

Houdini would be finished.

5 HARRY GETS A BREAK

January 30, 1899, St. Paul, Minnesota

It was an icy cold night, but inside the Palm Garden Beer Hall things were warming up. Groups of people were dotted around, some seated at tables and some wandering about. The air was smoky with candles and cigarettes, and over by the stage a man in striped shirt-sleeves was playing a piano.

A lady had just finished singing a song. She took a bow but hardly anybody noticed, before a little red-faced man hurried onto the stage. He was wearing a black suit and a red bow tie. He raised his hands to catch the audience's attention.

"And now . . ." he said, "all the way from Appleton, Wisconsin, by way of New York City, will you please welcome the Great Houdini!"

The piano player hit a few grand chords as Harry backed onto the stage carrying a table covered in magic stuff.

Harry didn't have many shows left before his year of performing was over. After that, he thought he'd end up **back at the necktie factory**. It was very sad, but for the time being, he was onstage and that was all that mattered.

Harry stepped to the front and clapped his hands a few times. It was so loud—almost like a gunshot—that people couldn't help turning around to watch him.

Harry glanced around the room. He'd done his tricks so many times that his hands worked automatically while he assessed the audience. It was the usual rabble, drinking, heckling, and hoping something would go wrong. But that night **one table was different**. There were three men staring at him, obviously from out of town. Harry didn't know what to make of them. He flicked a red silk handkerchief into the air and caught it in his hand. Then when he flicked it again, it turned green.

A few people clapped, but not the three men. Harry didn't care—he was more interested in their sharp suits. They were the exact style they wore in Chicago. These guys weren't drinking cheap beer either. As Harry flicked open a pack of cards, he was puzzled. What brought these guys to a **stinky beer hall 400 miles from home**? He could see them talking out of the corners of their mouths—it was just too bad he couldn't hear them!

Onstage Harry, sleeves rolled up, was making playing cards disappear from one hand and reappear in the other.

"He's good," said Mossy, the third man. "But I've seen a dozen like him."

Suddenly something smacked into the table, almost knocking a glass over. The three men gasped in surprise.

"It's a playing card!" said Joe. "Four of hearts."

Sure enough Harry was flicking cards the length of the room. Some people lept to catch them, and **one lady yelped** as the card hit her hand.

"He fires them off like bullets!" said Joe.

"He's good," Mossy said again. "But I've seen a dozen like him."

By then Harry was turning colored silks into little birds. It was clever, but the audience wasn't interested. They started to turn away and chat again.

"I've seen enough of this guy," Joe yawned. "I could use an early night."

"No, no, wait!" Martin said.

Onstage Harry was popping a dove away into a cage when he looked up for a moment and saw the chubby man waving at him.

"Mr. Houdini, sir!" Martin called. "Do you still escape from handcuffs?"

Harry was surprised, but delighted that the man seemed to know about him. "Indeed, sir, I do!" he said. "Would you like to see them?"

Harry picked up a solid looking pair, then hopped offstage and walked over to the table so that the three men could examine them.

"They look solid enough," Joe said.

"They don't fool me," Mossy said. "They'll have a secret little button or something to open them up. I've seen a dozen like them."

"Take a good look, gentlemen," said Harry. "If you can find a trick release, then I'll give you a hundred dollars."

"You got a hundred dollars?" Joe said.

"I don't need a hundred dollars," Harry said. "There's no trick."

Martin prodded and poked the cuffs before he passed them back. "They seem sound to me," he said.

"Then perhaps you'll join me on the stage, sir?" Harry suggested.

Onstage, Harry wiggled his fingers to show his hands were empty. Martin clamped the cuffs on Harry's wrists, then tugged them so that everybody could see they were tight. Harry asked Martin to cover his cuffed hands with a cloth. **The audience jeered suspiciously**.

"No way!" Martin said. "I guess your cloth has got a key or some secret little tool hidden in it."

"Oh, so you don't trust me?" Harry said. "Maybe you better borrow a cloth from the audience."

Several people offered things. Martin took a lady's scarf and draped it over Harry's hands so nobody could see what he was doing.

"Hmm," Harry said after a few seconds. "I gotta think about this."

With that **he took a free hand out from under the scarf and scratched his head**. The audience gave him a big laugh.

Martin was amazed. He snatched the scarf away completely. The empty handcuffs were dangling from Harry's little finger. Everyone laughed again, and Martin chuckled too. It was just what Harry wanted.

"I guess that's easy enough with your own cuffs," said Martin.

"My cuffs, your cuffs, ANY cuffs," Harry said defiantly. "NOTHING holds Houdini!"

The audience clapped and cheered as Martin returned to his seat.

"So what do you think, boys?" Martin asked. "Was this guy worth seeing?"

"That cuff-drop was the fastest I ever saw!" Joe said.

"I still say they're trick cuffs," Mossy said.

"I don't think so," Martin said. "Andy Rohan of the Chicago police force told me this Houdini guy can get out of anything they put on him."

"Anything?" Joe said.

"We'll find out tomorrow," Martin said. "Because we're going to come prepared!"

The next evening . . .

There was a big cheer as Harry was announced. He showed the audience his little square "ghost house" and invited two volunteers to check there were no hidden tools or keys inside.

Harry then asked Martin to come up and join him. If Harry was surprised at seeing the three different sets of handcuffs, he didn't show it.

"So which pair do you want to try first?" Martin said.

Harry took them and held them up one by one, and the audience gave each pair a little cheer. Then he passed them all back, rolled up his sleeves and held his bare arms out.

"Let's save time. **I'll take all three at once.**"

The audience watched in amazement as Martin bound Harry's wrists tightly together with all three sets. Martin dangled the keys in front of Harry.

"These are going in my pocket!" says Martin.

"That's fine by me," says Harry. "Now if you'll excuse me . . ."

He disappeared into his little ghost house and the flap shut behind him. The piano player started tinkling a well-known song and the audience sung along, but before they got to the second verse the ghost house opened.

Harry stepped out proudly holding the three sets of empty cuffs in one hand. He did a big bow and everyone applauded, except Mossy.

"Don't let him fool you!" he shouted to Martin. "The guy just disjointed his thumbs and squeezed the cuffs off. He doesn't unlock them at all."

"Is that right?" Martin asked Harry. "You don't actually unlock them?"

The audience began to murmur. Was Harry a cheat, or some sort of freak? Could he really scrunch his hands up small enough to slip free?

Harry smiled and shook his head. "I hope you've still got those keys," he said. "Because you're going to need them." He held the cuffs in the air, then let them drop so **they dangled down, linked in a chain**.

The audience whooped and cheered!

Joe gave Mossy a nudge. "So, wise guy, how did he do *that* without unlocking them?"

Mossy was still staring at the linked handcuffs. "No way," he said, shaking his head. "That is just not possible."

Onstage Martin shook Harry's hand. "Mr. Houdini, sir, my name is Martin Beck. We need to talk."

HARRY HITS THE HEADLINES

Martin Beck was looking for acts to appear in some of the **biggest and best** theaters in America. The Orpheum theaters (named after Orpheus, an ancient Greek musician who could charm the animals and trees with his music) all had grand interiors with velvet seats, the tickets were expensive, and the audience expected a night to remember!

Martin told Harry that if he dropped all his other magic tricks and just did handcuff challenges, he'd book Harry into one of his fancy theaters. Harry wasn't sure. Up until then he'd been having more success as the King of Cards than as the Wizard of Shackles, so he told Martin that he would only do escapes if he could do cards too.

"I'll think about it," said Martin, and he went back to Chicago.

Harry was really worried. Had he just **ruined his chance** of a big break? All he could do was hope for a message before he finished his run of shows at the Palm Garden. A whole week went by and he didn't hear anything, then another week, and then another until finally, one morning, he came in to work and found a telegram waiting for him.

Form 1204

CLASS OF SERVICE	SYMBOL
Telegram	
Day Letter	Blue
Night Message	Nite
Night Letter	N L

If none of these three symbols appears after the check (number of words) this is a telegram. Otherwise its character is indicated by the symbol appearing after the check.

WESTERN UNION TELEGRAM

NEWCOMB CARLTON, PRESIDENT   GEORGE W. E. ATKINS, FIRST VICE-PRESIDENT

CLASS OF SERVICE	SYMBOL
Telegram	
Day Letter	Blue
Night Message	Nite
Night Letter	N L

If none of these three symbols appears after the check (number of words) this is a telegram. Otherwise its character is indicated by the symbol appearing after the check.

Chicago, Mar. 14, '99

Houdini   Palmgarden, ... St. Paul Minn.

You can open Omaha March Twenty sixth—sixty dollars—will see act probably make you proposition for all next season.

M.Beck

That little piece of paper changed my whole life!

Twelve days later, Harry was four hundred miles away, walking onto the stage at the Orpheum Theater in Omaha. The $60 he got for the week was the most he'd ever been paid. For the first time he had a nice dressing room and a proper orchestra to play music when he came on. Harry was determined to make the most of it!

Every night he challenged people to bring their cuffs, locks, and chains, and every night he would slip free.

It had taken Harry eight tough years to make his breakthrough, but within two months he was suddenly a star. Everyone was talking about the Handcuff King. Martin Beck was so pleased that he arranged for Harry to tour all the other Orpheum theaters. **Harry's wages went up and up**, and—to top it off—Bess was happy to be back onstage with him.

Harry wanted everyone to know he was the BEST. So, in every city he visited, he put advertisements in the newspapers to announce how marvelous he was.

Why not? I WAS marvelous!

Some people who came to see his shows even complained that he spent more time talking about how good he was than doing the tricks!

The Ultimate Handcuff Escape

By June, Harry and Bess were appearing at the Orpheum in San Francisco. The fans loved Harry, but some other magicians were fed up of his constant bragging. One, calling himself Professor Benzon, was so agitated that he wrote a story for the paper saying that Harry wasn't anything special, because it was easy to open handcuffs by hiding a key in your mouth.

Harry was furious! He knew he had to prove the "professor" wrong, otherwise he and Bess would be laughed off the stage. There was only one thing for it . . .

Harry and Bess arranged a challenge at the City Hall police station. Harry **stripped completely naked** and a doctor checked him all over for any sort of hidden key. The police then slapped **ten pairs of handcuffs** on him, all crossed over and linked up with chains and hooked through a set of leg irons. Harry was weighed down by so much metal, he could hardly move. Bess gave him a kiss for luck, then four officers picked him up, carried him into an empty cell and shut the door.

Two minutes. That's all it took! Then Harry pulled the door open, heaved all the cuffs and chains out, and dumped them on the table.

The news of Harry's amazing naked escape traveled right across the country. He was quickly becoming a legend, but that wasn't quite the end of the story.

When Harry challenged Professor Benzon to try the same escape, he disappeared and never criticized Harry again!

HOW DID HARRY GEY OUT OF HANDCUFFS?

Harry had lots of ways of getting out of handcuffs that we know about, and probably lots more that we don't.

TRICK CUFFS

When Harry and Bess were doing the Metamorphosis, they used special trick handcuffs that might have a loose locking spring or a pin that came out, and they would ping open easily. One set nicely unlocked themselves if they were turned upside down!

Locked ...

CLICK!

... unlocked!

BORROWED CUFFS

When Harry was being put into somebody else's handcuffs, he always insisted the cuffs were locked and unlocked a few times before he put them on. This was to stop anyone fixing him up with cuffs that had to be sawn off. Even Harry couldn't chew through solid metal! He could also work out what he needed to do to get them off.

Harry knew what the inside of any set of handcuffs looked like. The simplest types would open if you just gave them a sharp tap in the right place. Harry might use the floor or a wall, or sometimes he even had a secret metal plate strapped to his leg inside his trousers.

For other types, he used a set of little picks. He often wore a belt with lots of tiny secret pockets, and as soon as he saw what he was going to need, he would slip the right pick into his hand.

If he had to strip completely naked, he could still hide the pick in his hair or his mouth. Sometimes when he was being chained up, he would offer to supply extra padlocks that looked normal, but had a secret panel with tiny tools inside!

One of his favorite tricks was to sneakily hook a pick onto the back of somebody's jacket! They'd search him, then he'd pinch his pick back and they'd be none the wiser!

Well, I can't find a key anywhere...

Ha ha! I bet you can't!

BENDY FINGERS

Harry had to be able to twist his fingers in any direction to get the keys into the most awkward holes. If he couldn't reach, he had to bend his whole body around to use his mouth and even his toes! He'd been practicing these contortions ever since he saw his first circus, and even though it could be very painful, Harry never gave up or lost his concentration.

THE MAGIC KISS

So how had Harry got the key in the San Francisco police cell when he was chained up, totally naked, and the doctor had checked his body? Simple. Bess had passed it over in her mouth when she kissed him!

Darby Handcuffs
(nicknamed Darbies by Scotland Yard!)

Ratchet Handcuffs

Bean Giant Handcuffs

Patrolman Handcuffs

6   Harry Heads Abroad

After his escape from the San Francisco police cell, everybody wanted to see the man the police couldn't hold, and Harry made the most of it! He did shows all along the East Coast of the United States, and every time he reached a new town **he would pull a spectacular stunt**; the newspapers would put it on their front pages and the theaters would be jam-packed with fans.

Most of Harry's stunts involved the police, who would make his escape as difficult as possible. They'd put Harry in several sets of handcuffs, then perhaps chain him to the wall of a prison cell and lock the door. It didn't matter what they did—minutes later he would be out again. He even got out of double-locked cell doors!

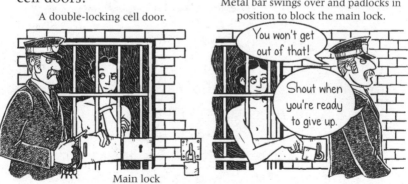

A double-locking cell door.

Metal bar swings over and padlocks in position to block the main lock.

You won't get out of that!

Shout when you're ready to give up.

Main lock

It had only taken Harry one year to go from nothing to being a national star. But now Martin Beck wanted him to become **an international star**!

THE MAN WHO MISSED THE BOAT

May 30, 1900, New York Harbor, New York

Harry and Bess were standing on the docks, all ready to get on board the SS *Kensington*. Martin Beck had arranged to send the Houdinis to London, along with a man called Richard Pitrot who had organized a theater tour for them.

Harry and Bess watched as their trunks and cases were loaded onto the ship, but **there was no sign** of this Pitrot man. All the other passengers were making their way up the gangplank, but Harry and Bess still waited. Suddenly a messenger boy ran from the booking hall with a telegram. Harry tore it open.

"Pitrot isn't coming," said Harry. "But he says all the shows are set up for us."

"Do we believe him?" asked Bess.

"Why shouldn't we?" said Harry. "Besides, we've got the tickets and the cases are on board. Let's just go!"

"If he's lying, we'll be stranded a long way from home," said Bess.

"Then it'll be an adventure," said Harry. "Come on!"

So Harry and Bess set sail and arrived in England ten days later. Harry's adventure hadn't started well. He had been **seasick almost the whole way** over, then when they started going around the theaters, it was bad news. There was nothing booked for him.

Hardly anybody had heard of Harry. He showed them all his newspaper cuttings, but **nobody wanted him**. This was London! They already had their own top performers, thank you. Harry needed to prove that he could pull crowds into the London theaters. After all, that's what theater managers wanted, and it was what he was best at!

He finally managed to fix a meeting at the grandest theater in London, the Alhambra in Leicester Square. The manager was named C. Dundas Slater and he wasn't interested in Harry or his newspaper cuttings, but Harry hadn't come all the way across the Atlantic Ocean just to be ignored!

"The only way you'll get me out of your office is if you take me to the police and have me locked up!" said Harry.

Mr. Slater happened to be friends with Superintendent Melville who ran **the most famous police station in the world**—Scotland Yard!

Ten seconds later . . .

> Lunch? Sounds good. Mind if this Yank comes too?

And that was how Harry ended up getting a week of shows at the Alhambra Theater in Leicester Square.

June 27, 1900, London, England

Word quickly got around London about the little American and his amazing escapes, but **some performers were jealous**. One of the first times Harry walked onto the stage he was rudely interrupted. A man with a big moustache lept from the audience claiming *he* was the real handcuff king. He called himself the Great Cirnoc, and said Harry was a fraud. But Harry knew just how to deal with him:

Cirnoc could have ruined Harry's London visit, but he made Harry look brilliant! Instead of a week, Harry ended up playing at the Alhambra for two months.

Harry Hits Europe

After his London shows had finished, Harry toured the rest of Britain, and then went over to Germany. The audiences there loved him, because he could speak German.

Though he was playing to packed theaters, the police were not impressed! In Germany you had to have a certificate to perform, and they refused to give Harry one—**they thought he was a cheat**!

September 20, 1900, Berlin, Germany

Harry was called to Berlin to do an escape in front of 300 top police officers. If he failed, he'd never be allowed to perform in Germany again.

Harry stripped down to his underpants, the police then taped his mouth shut and put him in two sets of leg irons. They put his hands behind his back and fixed them with several sets of cuffs and then trapped his thumbs together in a nasty little cuff called a thumbscrew! Finally they pulled a large sheet over Harry, and watched and waited.

Six minutes later he threw the sheet off, dumped all the metal and took a bow. Harry was NOT a cheat!

Although Harry was earning big money, he and Bess **never forgot what it was like to be poor**, so they always spent money carefully. A third-class train ticket would get you there just as quickly as first-class, so that's how Harry and Bess traveled. They usually stayed in cheap boarding houses too.

They weren't cheap, though! The Houdinis often held parties for the people who worked with them. Harry would tip porters and staff generously, and he often did free shows in children's homes, sometimes buying extra food and clothes for the children.

He would also try to track down great magicians of the past, visiting their widows or children to find out about them, even leaving flowers at their gravestones.

As always, Harry made sure that plenty of money went home to his mother in New York, and when one day he got a message to say Cecilia had booked a boat ticket and would join them in Germany a few months later, he was so excited!

HARRY THROWS A PARTY

Harry wanted his mom to have the perfect trip, so he and Bess made big plans. They had seen a fabulous dress in the window of a London clothing shop which had been **made for Queen Victoria**, though she had died without ever wearing it. Harry and Bess decided to buy it for Cecilia, so they went inside and asked the price. The shop manager wasn't interested. Harry and Bess didn't give up. They promised that the dress was only to be worn at a special private occasion that wasn't even going to happen in England, so what harm could it do?

Eventually the shop manager gave in, and Harry and Bess were ready to give Cecilia **the night of her life**!

Don't be ridiculous. Her Majesty's dress is not for sale! Absolutely no chance.

Cecilia arrived in Hamburg in April 1901. On that same night Harry's show was sold out, but he refused to go onstage until the theater had managed to fit an extra seat in for his mom. When Harry finished his run of shows, they took Cecilia back to her old homeland of Hungary, where **a big surprise** was waiting for her!

June 9, 1901, Budapest, Hungary

The Palm Court in the Royal Hotel was one of the finest rooms in the country. A large party of elderly guests had assembled. The ladies wore lace dresses with fancy hats and the gentlemen had cigars and dodgy whiskers. They were all whispering excitedly; some of them were even a bit nervous.

Harry had promised his father that he'd look after his mom, and he wanted all his mother's old friends to know that he'd kept his promise. He always said that the party in Budapest was **the happiest day of his life**!

HARRY GETS SOME HELP

Harry went on to do shows all around Europe, but within a year he was facing a big problem, especially in Germany. All the theaters were desperate to have him appear, but if they couldn't get him, they used **awful pretend Harrys**. These imposters used obvious fake handcuffs and trick chains, and made escapes look childish. Harry was furious. He worried that people would get fed up of escape acts and it would kill his trade.

But if Germany needed another escape artist, then Harry would supply one, and fortunately **he knew the perfect person** . . .

His little brother Dash was working as a magician back in New York. He was a very funny man, quite big and loud, and most importantly Harry knew he could be trusted. In November 1901 Harry called Dash over from America and fixed him up with exactly the same magic and escape equipment that he was using himself. Dash just needed a name . . .

And that's how two escape acts toured Germany and Harry didn't mind, because he was making money from both of them!

The Prison Truck

Harry and Bess's travels around Europe even took them to Russia, where everybody was terrified of the state police. The locals were desperate to see the man who had escaped from the police in other countries—could he escape from their own police as easily?

May 10, 1903, Moscow, Russia

Anxious not to be beaten, the Russian police set up Harry's toughest challenge yet. They put him into a Siberian transport truck—a metal cell on wheels used to carry the most dangerous criminals off to the far end of the country. Even though it was a freezing cold day, Harry was **stripped, inspected, chained, handcuffed, and locked inside**. The police all laughed and told him that the only key that could open the truck was hundreds of miles away in a Siberian prison. Bess then made sure that the police went to sit in their office so they couldn't see what Harry did.

The police didn't laugh forty-five minutes later when Harry knocked on their door. They rushed out and checked the truck. It was still locked and they had no idea how he'd gotten out! They were so

furious they banned Harry from telling anybody about it, but the story of the miracle escape soon got out and spread around the city. **Harry was everybody's hero**!

Harry almost certainly used some secret tools to get out of the truck, possibly smuggled inside a false sixth finger on his hand! But did he manage to reach out of the tiny barred window to pick the huge clunky door lock? Or did he remove a metal floor panel and then replace it? To this day, nobody knows!

The Mirror Handcuffs

March 17, 1904, London, England

A year after he visited Russia, Harry was back touring Britain, but business wasn't so good. Most police forces had gotten fed up of him breaking out of their prisons for publicity, and people were getting bored of his usual handcuff escapes. Then, late one night at the London Hippodrome, a man stepped onstage with a set of handcuffs **completely unlike anything** that anybody had seen before.

Harry took one look then passed them back. "These aren't normal cuffs," he said. "I already did two shows today, and it's late."

The crowd started to mutter and boo, then the stranger introduced himself.

"My name's Will Bennet and I'm from the *Daily Mirror* newspaper," he said. "These cuffs took five years to make. If you refuse to put them on, then you can never call yourself the Handcuff King again."

The Mirror Handcuffs

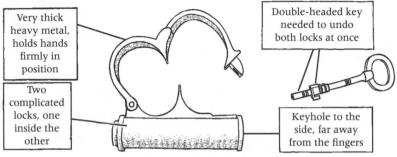

Very thick heavy metal, holds hands firmly in position

Double-headed key needed to undo both locks at once

Two complicated locks, one inside the other

Keyhole to the side, far away from the fingers

The audience was getting restless, and Harry looked uncomfortable. The Mirror handcuffs were by far **the most devious cuffs** he had ever seen, but he had no choice! Harry agreed to the challenge, but he announced that the theater would need to put on a special performance for him to do it.

For the next few days, the *Daily Mirror* advertised the event on its front pages, describing the handcuffs that "no mortal man" could escape from. London was buzzing with the story and five days later **4,000 people** crammed into the Hippodrome to see whether the great Harry Houdini would finally be beaten.

Will Bennet held up the handcuffs for all to see, then locked them firmly onto Harry's wrists. Harry went to hide in his little tent while the audience settled back and the orchestra played. Nobody expected anything to happen quickly!

After an hour, Harry came out of the tent looking very hot and tired. Everybody cheered, thinking he'd gotten the cuffs off, but he hadn't. He was just asking if the cuffs could be taken off for a moment so he could get rid of his jacket. Will refused, so Harry borrowed a penknife. He pulled the back of his jacket right over his head, then holding the knife with his teeth, he chopped it off! He went back into his tent, and after another hour, he staggered out waving the empty cuffs, and then collapsed.

The Handcuff King had won!

7   THE HOUSE THAT HARRY BUILT

When Harry got back from his first European tour in 1904, his mother, his brother Leopold, and his sister Carrie-Gladys were still living in a couple of cramped rooms in New York. But not for long!

Harry and Bess had saved up a lot of money during their four years abroad, and now they could put it to good use. Harry's family had always been important to him, and at last he could buy a big house where they could all live in comfort.

The house was number 278 on West 113th Street and it had four floors with a basement. It looked quite big from the outside, and it must have seemed even bigger on the inside because **it had twenty-six rooms**! Of course, it was much more than a house. It was Harry's headquarters, and he fitted it with all sorts of things to keep him busy and impress his guests!

As well as a trick front door and displays of magic equipment, the house also had several secret panels including one that opened behind a bookcase in his library. Even better, Harry was one of the first people to explore the uses of electricity, and he had his whole house **wired with microphones and speakers** so he could hear conversations in different rooms. He used this to pretend he could read people's minds, and he could even make voices come out of nowhere!

Harry's favorite room was his library on the top floor. This was where he escaped to when he wasn't exhausting himself with his tours and shows.

Harry's father had always loved collecting and studying books, and Harry was the same way. He had shelves and cupboards bursting with everything he could find written about magic, and he wrote several books and lots of magazine articles himself. If that wasn't enough, he kept in touch with other magicians, friends, politicians, policemen, lords and ladies, scientists, agents, and theater managers by writing about **100 letters a week**!

Harry hadn't stayed long enough at school to develop neat handwriting, so everywhere he went he took his trusty typewriter, and clattered away on it at all hours! He even invented special envelopes for his letters. If anyone tried to sneakily steam one open and seal it up again, the word "opened" would appear.

How Harry Kept Fit

Although Harry had lots of clever props, trick locks, secret keys, and magic apparatuses, by far his most important piece of equipment was his own body.

He was very careful with what he ate and drank. (At parties Bess liked champagne, but Harry stuck to water!) Early every morning he'd quietly get up and go to his workout room where he'd do four hours of exercises:

⭐ He would open the window, do lots of deep breathing and flex all his muscles, from his eyebrows right down to each one of his toes.

⭐ He'd do a full hour of push-ups, chin-ups, bench presses and all sorts of twisting and bending exercises. He would also practice his back flips and walk around on his hands a lot, a habit he'd kept going ever since he was nine.

⭐ He'd spend another hour in front of a giant mirror practicing fight moves such as box-ing, skipping, dodging, and high kicks.

⭐ He'd fill his giant bathtub with cold water, then lie in it and concentrate on slowing his heart rate, so he could stay face down without breath-ing for several minutes.

⭐ Finally he'd spend an hour doing his hand and foot exercises. He would flex his thumbs and fingers, endlessly making coins and cards flip and disappear, and at the same time he would be tying and undoing knots with his toes. Harry used muscles that most people don't even know they have!

When he finished, he'd tiptoe back into the bed-room to see if Bess wanted breakfast, but she'd still be fast asleep.

HARRY'S HOUSEMATES

CECILIA

Harry and Cecilia felt they had a real home for the first time since leaving Hungary, but even though Harry was a huge star, he was still a "mama's boy" and as a grown-up he would hug his mom and **even sit on her knee**.

You're getting a bit heavy now, Ehrich.

Harry had never forgotten the hard times when he was small—or his father's dying words to his mom, about Harry filling her apron with gold. He'd always taken them seriously. Now he was back in New York, his chance came! One night after a huge show he asked to be **paid in gold coins** and Harry finally made his father's last words come true.

LEOPOLD

Harry's youngest brother, Leopold Weiss, was one of the first doctors to experiment with X-rays. Harry was fascinated by anything to do with his body, so he volunteered to be X-rayed lots of times. Sometimes he'd swallow things to see where they'd go to, and then use the old circus trick to bring them up again. In those days nobody knew how dangerous X-rays could be, so Harry was very lucky not to be seriously affected.

BESS

If you're going to marry someone who risks his life nearly every day, you do have to be a bit bonkers. Bess was perfect for the job. She used to worry a lot, but she also had a fierce temper and would kick and scream at Harry, who'd storm out of the house. When he came back he'd toss his hat in through the door. If the hat flew out again he knew he had to go for a longer walk!

As Bess got older, she stopped performing, but she was always around to make sure Harry was safe. **She believed in theater ghosts and superstitions**! Bess never wore anything yellow because it might bring Harry bad luck while he was onstage and she refused to go into the dressing room if she thought somebody had whistled in it—because it was supposed to make the scenery fall down!

CARRIE-GLADYS

Harry's little sister spent most of her life living with Cecilia. Being almost blind didn't stop her joining in the fun!

April 11, 1905, Cardiff, Wales

A year after Harry had bought the house, he was back in Britain for a few months. Harry couldn't possibly appear at all the venues that wanted him, and some of the places he missed got very upset about it.

The Cardiff Empire offered Harry £125 for a week of shows (about $19,000 today). When he chose the King's Theater down the road instead because they offered £150 (about $23,000 today), the Empire was furious. To get their own back, the Empire put on a man called Frank Hilbert, who **called Harry a cheat** and claimed to give away all his secrets.

It was never a good idea to upset Harry.

One evening Harry snuck into the audience disguised as an old man, he then stood up and started heckling. Three strong ushers grabbed him and threw him out, but they hadn't expected Dash to be there too and soon they were all having a fight in the street. Harry and Dash staggered away, just in time for Harry to get onstage at the King's Theater.

Meanwhile back at the Empire, Frank thought his troubles were over, until two ladies got up. They waved some handcuffs and challenged Frank to get out of them. When he refused, **the audience booed him off** and the whole town heard about it!

Of course the newspapers loved the story. Harry loved it too, because it had all gone just as he'd planned. The two mysterious ladies were . . . Bess and his little sister Carrie-Gladys, who had joined them on the tour!

8 HARRY GETS DANGEROUS

Although Harry had spent his first year of fame in America, he'd spent most of the next four years in Europe. While he'd been away, lots of other people had been touring America with escape acts. Harry didn't seem so special anymore and American theaters wouldn't offer the big money he'd gotten used to.

Harry wasn't having that! He badly needed a blast of publicity to remind everybody he was still the BIG STAR, so he decided to do **something sensational**. He tracked down a young imitator who had the nerve to call himself "Jacques Boudini" and challenged him to a death-defying escape.

September 20, 1905, New York, New York

The two men met on a tugboat on the Hudson River. They were both handcuffed and put into ankle shackles, then each had a rope tied around his waist. They were going to jump into the river, then whoever got out first would win $500 from the loser!

Of course Harry had made sure that the boat was packed with newspaper reporters, and there were crowds all along the riverside. Jacques looked terrified, but **Harry just gave him a cold stare**.

KA-SPLOSH! In they went and the weight of the metal pulled them both straight under the water. The river was about **thirty-three feet deep**!

A minute passed and then Harry popped up and threw his handcuffs onto the boat.

"Is Boudini up yet?" he asked, paddling with his hands to keep afloat.

"No!" everybody shouted.

Harry slipped back under, just as Jacques splashed his way to the top and gulped some air. His hands were still cuffed and he wasn't looking very happy! He took a deep breath and went under again.

A minute later Harry stuck one leg up out of the water to show he'd gotten it free. A few seconds after that he was climbing onto the tug holding the empty shackles, with cheers from the crowd ringing in his ears!

Meanwhile, Jacques was hauled out of the water and laid on the deck of the boat coughing up salty river water and still **completely locked up**. Harry had won his bet!

The next day, he was splashed all over the front pages. Once again, everyone was talking about Harry and theaters were begging him to appear, so it was lucky that Jacques had accepted the bet, wasn't it?

Well, nobody knew this at the time, but it turns out that **Jacques and Harry had been friends for quite a few years**. Harry wasn't just a brilliant performer, he was also an expert at advertising himself. So had Harry planned the whole challenge and paid Jacques to lose so he could make himself famous again?

If so, it worked!

HARRY CHEATS THE GALLOWS!

January 6, 1906, Washington, DC

One good stunt was only worth a few weeks' fame, so Harry had to keep coming up with new ideas to keep the newspapers interested. The public loved gruesome crime stories, so **what if he was to escape from Murderers' Row** in Washington DC's federal jail?

The worst prisoners spent their last days there, and the cells had the thickest walls, heaviest doors, and most complicated locks. The papers wanted to know: if Harry had been a murderer, could he have escaped the gallows?

Harry was stripped and locked in a cell with a man who only had days to live. The guards and the news reporters went back to the office and waited. Sure enough, within twenty one minutes Harry had gotten out and joined them. They'd all known he would escape somehow, so they weren't all that surprised, until Harry said . . .

"By the way, I let all your other prisoners out too!"

For a few seconds **there was total panic**!

"But don't worry, I locked them all up again."

The warders dashed to check Murderers' Row and were relieved to see the prisoners were locked up—but Harry had put them all back in the wrong cells! (Harry had asked the prisoners if they wanted to make the warders look foolish—of course they agreed!)

March 20, 1906, Boston, Massachusetts

The newspapers loved the mixed-up murderers story, but two months later Harry went on to do his cleverest escape ever, from a prison called the Boston Tombs.

86

In addition to Harry's usual lock-picking skills, he had managed to vault over the prison wall where he had arranged a car to pick him up. However, the most amazing part of the escape is how fast he did it!

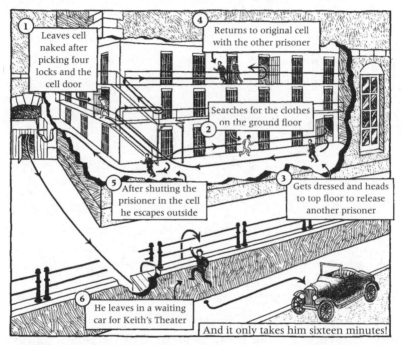

1. Leaves cell naked after picking four locks and the cell door
2. Searches for the clothes on the ground floor
3. Gets dressed and heads to top floor to release another prisoner
4. Returns to original cell with the other prisoner
5. After shutting the prisoner in the cell he escapes outside
6. He leaves in a waiting car for Keith's Theater

And it only takes him sixteen minutes!

HARRY TAKES THE PLUNGE

Later that year, Harry had a really bad night at a theater in Detroit. A local magician tried to ruin the show by sabotaging the handcuffs. It took Harry **nearly two hours** to get them off. He was really upset and got even more upset when the theater manager asked to see him.

"Everyone says you're getting boring, Harry," he said. "If I can't sell tickets, I'll have to cancel your show."

Harry was incensed. **Nobody called the great Houdini boring**! He'd spent years building up his reputation, and now it was about to be ruined by one pair of dodgy handcuffs. He had to get the public back on side, and fast, or he was finished. His last river escape had worked really well, so he decided to do one that was even more dangerous!

November 27, 1906, Detroit, Michigan

The day was bleak with snow in the air, and Harry was standing high up on the railings of Belle Isle Bridge. He had promised the newspapers a stunt that Detroit would never forget. It was lunchtime and crowds had gathered along the banks of the river. They were all wrapped up, warm in their coats and boots, but Harry was just wearing a swimsuit and two pairs of the latest police handcuffs.

The people couldn't believe it! Was he really going to leap off the bridge with those heavy iron shackles around his wrists? **The river was freezing**! It would be like jumping off the top of a house into a pool of ice.

Harry was taking slow deep breaths to calm his pulse rate and maximize his body temperature. When he'd announced he was going to do this jump, he hadn't known it was going to be so cold, but there was no backing out now!

Whatever happened, he knew he had to make the most of it, so to get the newspapers even more excited,

he borrowed an old envelope from one of the reporters and scribbled on the back.

It was Harry's will—in case he didn't survive!

Down on the river two people in a little row boat were ready to fish him out. The police had checked the handcuffs, and everyone had moved a few steps back. Harry had been taking cold baths every morning, so could hitting that river be so much worse? There was only one way to find out.

Harry jumped.

There was a loud gasp from the crowd as he fell with his hands locked together.

SPLOOSH!

He disappeared under the water.

The cold cut through Harry like a knife, but he knew above all else that he had to STAY CALM. In the water, his left hand quickly cramped up and felt as dead as a lump of ice. He was sinking down deep but all his concentration was spent on keeping his right hand working. The cuffs had a new type of lock, and **Harry had to feel his way around with frozen fingers**. No good!

Harry kicked his feet and came up for air. The water lapped around his face and down he went again. Once more he tapped and twiddled. His lungs were bursting, his head was going woozy, but at last the first pair of cuffs came loose, quickly followed by the second. He fought his way back up to the surface and, using his good arm, he swam for the boat.

The crowd on the bridge went wild. Once again everybody was calling him the greatest showman on earth!

WHO HELPED HARRY?

As the shows and audiences got bigger, Harry needed a team of assistants to help him. It was a demanding job! It wasn't well paid, and Harry would often wake up in the night with an idea and expect his assistants to get up. When things went well, there were parties and presents, but Harry also had a sharp temper! Luckily Bess was always there to smooth things over. She would take Harry aside to let off steam, and make sure his team got time off or she'd slip them some extra money if they needed it.

Working for Harry might have been tough, but it was never boring!

9 HARRY'S DEATH-DEFYING MYSTERIES!

Harry's river jump in Detroit had gotten him so much attention that he repeated it in several other cities as he toured America. Huge crowds would line the riverbanks to watch him, but if people could see him risking his life for free, why should they pay to see him twiddling around with handcuffs onstage? **Ticket sales for his theater shows started to fall again**.

Harry needed to drag the people back into the theaters with a new trick that looked just as dangerous as the river jumps.

How about squeezing myself into a metal milk can full of water, with the lid padlocked shut?

THE MILK CAN ESCAPE

The audience was whispering and giggling as the theater suddenly went dark. There was a long drum roll, then a loud voice boomed:

"Ladies and gentlemen, we proudly present the international master of escape, the handcuff king, the defier of death, the one and only Houdini!"

Dramatic music played as the stage lit up and Harry stepped out in front of the curtains. The audience applauded wildly. Oh boy, they couldn't wait to see what he was going to do!

For a few moments Harry looked out into the audience with his piercing eyes. This was all part of the show! Everyone started to feel guilty. They might not have admitted it, but **they had all come to see if he was going to drown**. Then Harry smiled and said hello, and everyone felt they could relax a bit. What they didn't realize was that through his expert showmanship, Harry was starting to take complete control over everything they were thinking and feeling!

Harry said how nice it was to be there, and how last time the police tried to lock him up but he escaped and how he had toured all over Europe and Russia (in fact, he talked an awful lot about himself), and then he said he was going to perform the greatest mystery ever presented on a stage by anybody anywhere in the whole world.

The curtains opened. There, in the middle of the stage, was an ugly-looking metal can that seemed hardly big enough to hold him.

Harry gave the can a kick to show how solid it was. Then he invited two local volunteers up to check for secret panels and move the can around the stage to make sure there wasn't a trap door underneath.

Once the volunteers were back in their seats, Harry waved at the orchestra, the music started, and he went offstage. Meanwhile, two assistants filled the can up with buckets of water. Harry came back on wearing a bathing suit, and everybody shivered nervously. They realized that Harry really WAS going to do this!

Harry's assistants helped him climb into the can, and some water sploshed out over the top. Before the proper trick started, he invited the audience to get a feel of what being underwater was like. **He asked everyone to take a deep breath** with him and hold it, then his head disappeard down inside the can. One of the assistants filled the can up with more water so everyone knew that Harry wasn't cheating.

The orchestra played a steady low beat and a large stopwatch on the stage counted the seconds as everyone held their breath. After half a minute people started gasping and spluttering, and soon everybody had given up. **Harry was still in there**! It was well over a minute before he stood up, shook the water off his head and smiled at everyone.

"And now," Harry said, "I, the great Houdini, will demonstrate the most marvellous mystery of the age!"

Harry held out his hands, so an assistant could slap on a set of handcuffs. Then he closed his eyes, took a full, deep breath, and disappeared back down into the can.

Harry's assistants sprung into action. They quickly filled the can up again, then slammed the heavy lid down and snapped on the six padlocks. All six keys were put on a table at the side where everyone could see them.

One of the assistants pulled a curtain all the way around the can and then they all stood back. Harry was in there, on his own, and **he couldn't breathe**.

The audience waited … and waited … and waited …

A full minute passed. Everyone was still staring at the curtain but nothing had happened. One of the assistants at the side of the stage was checking the giant stopwatch and looked a bit nervous.

A minute and a half went by. The whole audience was getting uneasy. Why hadn't Harry come out?

The seconds ticked by; each one seemed slower and more painful than the last.

After one minute, fifty five seconds, the two assistants glanced nervously at the curtain. Should they interfere? Some of the audience were getting anxious and shouted for them to go in.

Two minutes and five seconds had gone by when suddenly Harry burst through the curtain. He was dripping with water, gasping for breath, but he was alive!

The whole theater cried with relief, but Harry had another surprise for them! He pulled back the curtain to show the milk can was sitting exactly as they last saw it, with all six padlocks still holding the lid down.

The applause was deafening! Harry took a deep bow. Once again he had proved that he was the greatest showman on earth!

How Did He Do It?

As soon as Harry started doing his milk can escape, his shows began selling out again. Everyone was baffled as to how he got out, but they would have been even more surprised to know it actually only took him five seconds! Harry would wait another two minutes behind the curtain before stepping out—but why?

Because I was putting on a show! I wanted everyone to be REALLY WORRIED, so they'd be all the happier to see me escape!

It's true. If he'd gotten out too quickly, the trick would have looked too easy. There's a story that one time Harry read a newspaper while he waited . . .

But how did he get out?

There are different versions of this trick, but all of them rely on one secret—the top with all the padlocks comes off!

Shhh, Harry! They'll hear you turning the pages!

MILK CAN with false outer collar to fix padlocks

Lid in place

Padlocks fixed to false collar

Lid and false collar can be lifted off from inside

The false collar was quite heavy and it was held in place by a secret fastening on the inside of the can, so it would have been impossible to detect without actually climbing inside. All Harry had to do was release the fastening and push it off.

It all sounds very easy but you had to be very strong and fit to do the trick! Harry's brother Dash performed it too, but one time he squeezed in and got cramps, then fainted. He had to be cut out by the stage crew before he drowned!

HARRY FLIES DOWN UNDER!

The news of Harry and his milk can escape gradually spread around the world, and he was invited to Australia. At first he refused, because he didn't want to leave his mom, but after talking it over with Bess, in 1910 Harry finally decided to take the once-in-a-life-time chance. One thing really helped him make his mind up . . .

They were going to pay me for 12 weeks of shows as well as an extra 12 weeks to travel and have fun!

Harry took some unusual cargo on the boat with him—**an airplane**! Flying was the latest craze and he'd been having lessons in Germany. Airplanes attracted a lot of publicity and money and Harry loved both!

When he found out that nobody had ever flown in Australia before, he couldn't resist. He had to wait for the right conditions before he was able to take off, but he managed to stay in the air for a few minutes then land neatly, becoming **the first person ever to fly over Australia** . . . well, a very small part of it!

HARRY'S SMALLEST-EVER AUDIENCE

Harry thrilled people with his milk can for years, but a lot of performers copied it, and Harry felt cheated. He knew he had to invent an even better trick that nobody could possibly copy. This resulted in one of the strangest shows he ever performed!

April 29, 1911, Southampton, England

Harry was onstage in a little theater, in a play called *Houdini Upside Down*. For the highlight of the show, he appeared in a bathing suit. A pair of solid wooden stocks were lowered down from above and his feet were locked into them.

The stocks were hoisted back into the air, leaving Harry upside down, dangling by his ankles.

Next came the really nasty bit.

Harry was quickly lowered head-first into a tall glass tank filled with water. His hair was swirling about and **there was absolutely no way he could breathe.** The stocks were locked onto the top of the tank and then a curtain was pulled around it. After a couple of minutes, Harry stepped out from behind the curtain, dripping wet.

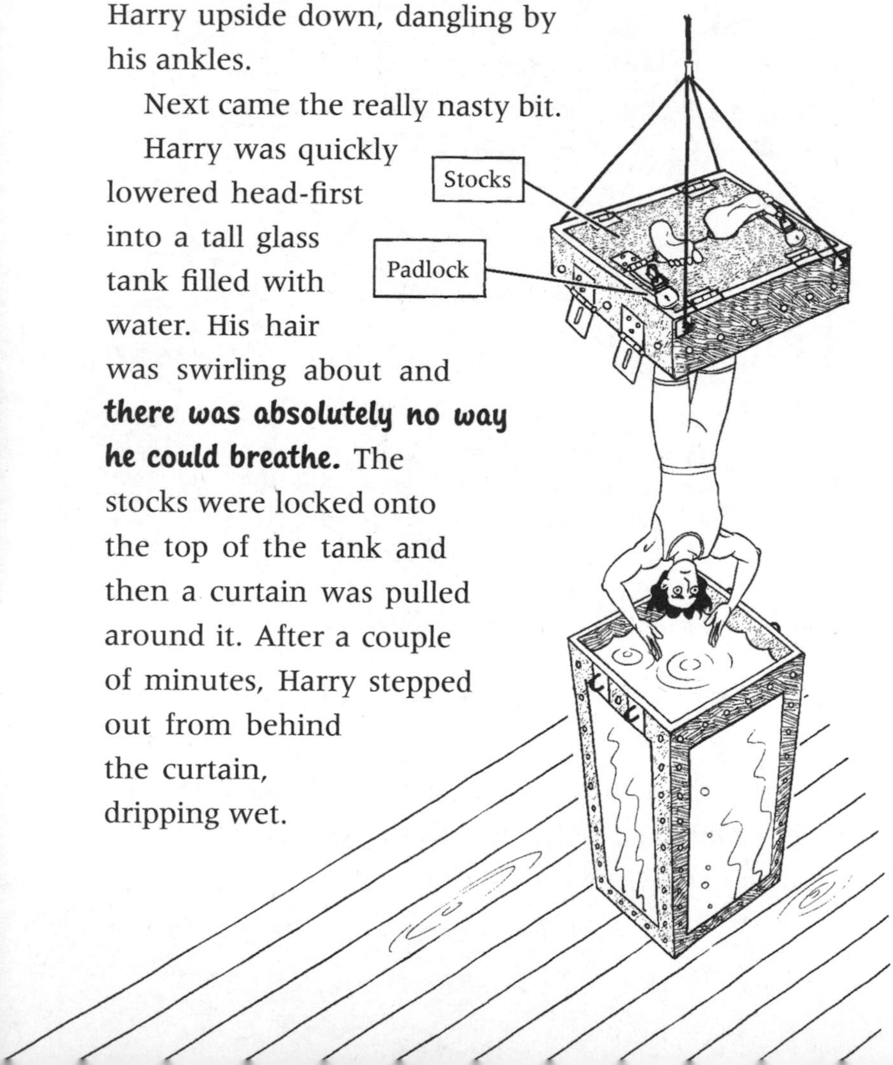

Stocks

Padlock

Here's the strangest part—this little play was only ever performed once, and **there was only one person in the audience**! So what was going on?

Harry had spent over three years designing the water tank, and it had cost over $10,000 to build (about $322,000 today). He was going to use it to thrill people all over the world, and this time he'd worked out an ingenious way of stopping anybody pinching his idea.

Although there was no law against stealing tricks, you weren't allowed to perform a play without getting permission from the author. Harry had written this little play, and even though only one person ever saw it, that was enough for him to claim he had the copyright. If anybody did try to steal his tank trick, he could sue them for quite a lot of money!

That'll show them!

THE CHINESE WATER TORTURE CELL

Harry knew the water tank escape was going to be **massive**, so he wanted to make sure he got everything about it exactly right. It took him over a year to plan its first proper performance.

September 21, 1912, Berlin, Germany

The Chinese Water Torture Cell was a name that would grab people's attention. Harry made sure the poster had a really freakish picture too.

People would actually see him trapped upside down in the water! He offered $1,000 to anyone who could prove that he could somehow get air to breathe at the bottom of the tank. It was irresistible, and the audiences flocked to see it.

Harry always invited volunteers onstage to inspect the tank. He would bang the glass to show that it was all very heavy and solid, and let the volunteers push the tank around the stage to make sure it wasn't sitting on a secret trap door. They could even lock his feet into the stocks.

When Harry had been lifted above the tank, he would **ask the audience to hold their breath** until they saw him again. Then he would be lowered into the tank and locked upside down in the water. He would twist and turn to show there wasn't much space to move, and the audience would all be chewing their knuckles with worry. When the curtain went around the tank, the orchestra would play "Asleep in the Deep"—a well-known song about a couple who had drowned!

After about a minute, everybody would have given up holding their breath. They would all be staring at the curtain, expecting Harry to burst out . . . but then one of the assistants would pull the curtain aside. The audience would shriek with horror, because **Harry was still upside down** in the water, clawing at the glass!

The curtain would drop back into place and the assistants might bring on an axe to make people think something had gone wrong. But of course it was all for show. Harry would already be out of the tank and standing behind the curtain, waiting for exactly the right moment to burst through and put everyone out of their misery.

The Chinese Water Torture Cell was the perfect trick for Harry! It was far more than just a dramatic escape—it also gave him **complete control** over his audience. He could make them feel terrified one moment and weep with relief the next!

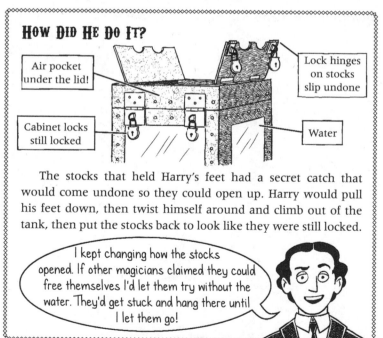

How Did He Do It?

Air pocket under the lid!

Lock hinges on stocks slip undone

Cabinet locks still locked

Water

The stocks that held Harry's feet had a secret catch that would come undone so they could open up. Harry would pull his feet down, then twist himself around and climb out of the tank, then put the stocks back to look like they were still locked.

I kept changing how the stocks opened. If other magicians claimed they could free themselves I'd let them try without the water. They'd get stuck and hang there until I let them go!

There was also a second secret. Although the tank had water right to the top, the lid was full of air. As soon as the curtains first closed, Harry would free his feet, twist himself around to breathe, then get back in time for everyone to see him upside down again. The second time the curtains closed, he would twist around and get himself out.

It sounds quite simple, doesn't it? Don't kid yourself. **You couldn't do it**.

The most important thing about the trick is that Harry was very fit and very strong and he'd practiced for years being underwater, upside down, curling up, twisting, turning, holding his breath, and above all staying calm. For anyone else who hadn't done the training, this trick might be the last thing they ever tried to do.

AN UNWANTED TELEGRAM

It seemed that nothing could go wrong for Harry. He was being invited all over the world to perform for huge amounts of money, but whenever he and Bess got on board a train or a steamship to leave New York, there was always a moment he hated: he had to **say goodbye** to his mom! Cecilia always came to see him off. Harry would hug her and kiss her until the very last second when it was time to jump aboard, and then he would wave until she was long out of sight. He did this every time, and every time she was a little bit older and Harry was a little bit more worried about her.

In July 1913 Cecilia was seventy-two. Harry and Bess had sailed over to Hamburg, and traveled on to Copenhagen where Harry was set to do a show for the Danish royal family. They had only just arrived when Harry got a transatlantic telegram. In those days long-distance telegrams were rare and expensive, and even before Harry opened it, **he must have guessed the worst**. Cecilia had suffered a stroke and died two days earlier.

Harry was wrecked, unable to go on. His bookings were cancelled and they returned to New York as soon as they could. Although Jewish tradition says a body must be buried immediately, the family agreed to delay the burial so Harry could see his beloved mother one last time.

Harry went back to doing his shows, but he was just turning up, performing, then going back to the hotel and collapsing in tears. Some people believed in his mysterious powers so much that they even asked Harry if he could do something to bring his mother back.

Of course he couldn't. With all his amazing skills, that was one trick that even poor Harry couldn't perform. But what if there was some way that he could talk to her again? It was a thought that would keep him occupied for the rest of his life.

10 HARRY HANGS UPSIDE DOWN

Harry first performed his Chinese Water Torture Cell to his smallest-ever audience, but now we'll find out how Harry got his BIGGEST-ever audience!

Before his mom died, Harry had often talked about retiring from performing to concentrate on his books and magic studies, but after she'd gone he found he needed the **thrills and distraction** of his live events even more. He always told people how brilliant he was, but this was partly to push himself even harder. Of course his big-headed attitude didn't always go down well, especially with some of his rival magicians.

To maintain his reputation, Harry had to keep giving the newspapers even bigger and more sensational stories. The prison escapes and river jumps had been really successful, so now he planned **a new big outdoor event** using an item that he'd discovered nearly twenty years before. It was only now that he realized quite how spectacular he could make it!

A Trip to the Asylum

Back in the days when Harry was performing with the medicine shows, a doctor had given him a tour of the local insane asylum. When they came to a locked door with a small barred window, Harry looked through and saw a patient lying on the floor. He was wrapped up in a strange outfit that Harry had never seen before.

"It's a straightjackct," said the doctor. "It holds his arms around his body so that he can't hurt himself or anyone else."

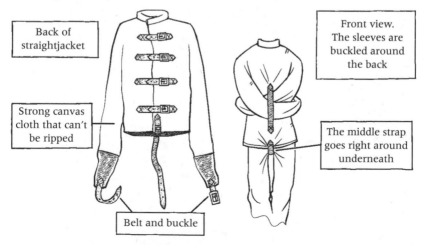

Back of straightjacket

Front view. The sleeves are buckled around the back

Strong canvas cloth that can't be ripped

The middle strap goes right around underneath

Belt and buckle

Thankfully we have much kinder ways of restraining people these days, but back then a straightjacket was the best option.

Suddenly the poor man started having a fit. He was screaming and grunting and thrashing about, but the jacket was holding him tight.

Anybody else would have felt sorry for the patient, but **Harry had other things on his mind . . .**

He can't get out of it, but I bet I could.

In 1913 Harry got his own straightjacket, and for the next week he hardly slept as he worked out the best way to get it off. The ends of the sleeves were sewn up, so his nimble fingers were no use to him. Instead he had to rely on his incredible strength, plus his contortion skills, bending his arms at impossible angles so he could **reach the buckles with his teeth**. Harry had also learned to "expand himself," so that when the jacket was being put on him he could swell out his chest and stomach muscles to make himself as big as possible. Then when he was escaping he would shrink down to make a bit of free space inside the jacket.

Sometimes he had to dislocate his shoulder to get free. That meant **pulling his arm bone right out of its socket** so he could slip himself around inside the jacket, then popping it back in again. And yes, it was REALLY painful, but one way or another, Harry always managed to get out of it.

MAKING A GOOD TRICK BETTER

When Harry first performed the straightjacket escape, the audiences didn't like it. It took far too long and he used to hide inside his ghost house so they couldn't watch what he was doing. However, when Dash tried performing the same escape, he realized it was far better to let people watch him. Harry was horrified that his secrets might be revealed, but Dash assured him the audience would love it and all they'd see would be him squirming around.

Dash was right. But the straightjacket still wasn't a headline trick. Harry needed to do something else to make it better, and he got the idea when he visited a young fan in Sheffield in 1914. The boy showed him his own version of the straightjacket escape—**hanging upside down** from a beam in his bedroom!

Being upside down actually made it easier for Harry to work some more free space inside the jacket. Eventually he got his escape time down to a couple of minutes. All it needed now was Harry's imagination to make this into one of the **most sensational** stunts of all time . . .

April 19, 1916, Washington, DC

"Houdini to Hang" was such a brilliant advertisement that 100,000 people gathered in the streets to watch.

The whole crowd was staring upwards with their mouths wide open! High above them, the tiny figure of Harry was silhouetted against the sky. Moments before, he'd been on a stage in front of them. They'd seen the straps of his straightjacket yanked and buckled so roughly that Harry had nearly been pulled over as he was fastened into it. His feet had been tied together and then hooked onto a thick rope which stretched up to a pulley arm sticking out of the very top of a nearby building.

His assistants had held Harry's shoulders as the rope was reeled in, his feet were pulled above his head and soon he was hanging upside down like a fish on a very long line. Then up he went past all the windows, **tied up and helpless as a sausage**, dangling on the end of the rope and swaying slightly as he went.

The crowd could hardly breathe until he stopped at the twelfth floor.

Wait a minute, they've hung him up the wrong way around!

When Harry had been put into the straightjacket, he had expanded his muscles and braced his arms, but by now he was relaxed again so that the jacket was slightly looser around him.

He would be flexing his feet and toes to ensure his blood kept moving, otherwise it would have rushed down to his head and he would have **blacked out**. He couldn't stop himself spinning, so one moment he would be facing the building about six feet away, and the next he would be looking down the street far below as it stretched off into the distance, jammed with people looking as tiny as matchsticks. The noise from the crowd would drift up and be lost against the wind in his ears and the creaking of the rope holding his feet. Harry was very high and completely alone, but none of that mattered, because it was time to go to work . . .

Suddenly Harry's body started bending and twisting as he threw himself about. The crowd groaned and roared; some covered their faces, unable to watch. If the rope broke or his feet slipped out, there was no safety net—it would mean a long drop to a **certain death**. But Harry's arms were getting looser and soon he curled up and managed to jerk the long sleeves over his head. He heaved and pushed the jacket down over his shoulders, and suddenly he was free.

He waved the jacket around, then let it drop. No one could take their eyes off the jacket as it fell past all the windows with the sleeves flapping around. Is that what Harry would have looked like if he'd fallen? Eeek!

As Harry's assistants scooped the jacket from the street, everyone looked up again to see Harry pull himself up on the rope and do an upside-down bow . . . and every single one of the 100,000 people watching told their children and grandchildren about it for the rest of their lives!

Of course Harry hit the headlines and the public loved him, but, perhaps best of all, his jealous rivals could only weep.

11 THE SEA MONSTER AND OTHER SENSATIONS!

Once, when Harry was escaping from a wooden box dropped in a river, the trick went horribly wrong. The box landed sideways in the mud at the bottom and Harry couldn't open the secret panel! Even though he was deep down with the muddy water blinding him, he had to stay calm so that he didn't waste his breath, and then rock the box until it tipped over and he could get out.

You'd think this would have put Harry off his escapes, but it didn't. He was prepared to get out of almost anything.

Sometimes he invited local firms to come onstage and build a solid wooden packing case around him, so everybody knew there would be no secret panels or dummy bolts! Once Harry was out, the case would look completely untouched.

He also escaped from glass tanks, iron boxes, coffins, boilers, barrels, cages, and graves. In 1907 he even escaped from a **giant paper envelope** sealed up all the way along the top. This might not sound especially difficult, but he got out of the envelope without ripping it, tearing it, or breaking the seal!

But far stranger than all the others was Harry's escape from a sea monster!

September 26, 1911, Boston, Massachusetts

A huge creature had washed up dead on a beach near Boston. Everybody was talking about it, but nobody knew what it was. Harry described it as a mix between a whale and an octopus. He knew the newspapers would love his idea . . .

DAILY HERALD
GIANT SEA MONSTER
—HOUDINI'S GREATEST CHALLENGE YET!

NEWS NEWS NEWS!
CAN HOUDINI DEFY DEATH FROM DEEP SEA DEVIL?

On the morning of the show, the creature was paraded through the streets on a truck. Thousands turned out to watch it arrive at Boston's biggest theater, where it was **cut open onstage**. Harry had his arms and legs cuffed and

was helped into the belly of the beast. They put a breathing tube in his mouth, then sewed the beast up and wrapped it in chains. Finally a curtain was pulled around the whole thing.

Inside was pitch black. Harry was squashed in on all sides by cold wet fishy stuff and the smell . . . URGHHH!

But fifteen minutes later, Harry appeared onstage, and of course the packed theater went wild. What's more, when they drew back the curtain, **the beast was still chained up**. Nobody ever knew for sure how he got out.

HARRY'S BIGGEST-EVER TRICK

January 7, 1918, New York, New York

In June 1917 Harry was elected head of the Society of American Magicians (SAM). The United States had just joined the war against Germany and Harry wanted to sign up for the US Army and fight for the country he was so proud of. Sadly he was forty-three and too old, so instead he encouraged the society members to help in any way they could. The magicians used their special skills to come up with new types of camouflage, codes, ways of sending secret messages, and spy gadgets. Harry cancelled all his planned shows and toured army camps, entertaining the troops. He also gave lectures to soldiers on how to free themselves if they were tied up, and showed them some of the handcuffs and chains he'd escaped from on his German tours.

Above all, Harry organized fundraising events with all the major stars of the day. These shows were huge, and many of them were put on at the 5,000-seat

New York Hippodrome—the biggest stage in the world. Its orchestra had 125 players, and it even **had its own zoo**, which gave Harry the idea for his biggest-ever trick!

Onstage with Harry was a huge cabinet on wheels, about the size of a small garage. One end of the cabinet had a round, barred window in the middle. The other end had tall double doors that were wide open. Inside, it was pitch black and empty.

"Ladies and gentlemen!" cried Harry. "Will you please welcome my very special guest . . . Jennie!"

When Jennie came on, the whole audience rose to their feet and cheered. If you'd been there you would have cheered too. Jennie had a pretty ribbon around her neck, a bracelet around her leg, and she weighed five tons. She ran right around the stage, her feet thumping and bashing as she went, then she stopped next to Harry and gave him a big kiss with her trunk. (Actually, she was helping herself to some sugar cubes Harry was holding, but let's not be fussy.)

Ha ha, thank you Jennie!

HOORAY!

Harry had promised to make a real living, breathing elephant vanish before their very eyes! **The audience couldn't believe it**. Twelve stagehands lowered a ramp down from the cabinet doors and Jennie's trainer led her inside. When the doors were closed, they created another round window showing the inside of the cabinet. The audience could still see Jennie. Harry pulled the curtains over the windows at either end, then the stagehands heaved the whole cabinet around so the end with just the window faced the audience. Harry clapped his hands and the curtains at both ends were opened. The audience could see through to the light shining in the window at the far end. Jennie had disappeared!

SO WHERE DID JENNIE GO?

She was tucked into the side of the cabinet with a black cloth over her! It sounds obvious, but the trick could only have worked on the massive Hippodrome stage. The cabinet was larger than it looked, and the windows were carefully placed so that nobody in the audience could get a clear view through them. A bright light shining in from behind made the back window look bigger than it actually was. Don't underestimate how clever this illusion was—thousands of people were completely fooled by it!

HARRY IN HOLLYWOOD!

Harry was prepared to try anything, so he was thrilled in 1915 when he was asked to star in the movie *20,000*

Leagues Under the Sea. The silent film industry was just getting going and **Harry was very tempted**, until he found out that they weren't going to pay him as much as he thought he was worth.

Instead he came up with his own ideas, and in 1918 they were turned into a film called *The Master Mystery*. Cinemas showed it in fifteen twenty-minute episodes (a bit like an early TV series). Harry played secret agent Quentin Locke, who was always saving ladies in distress and stopping evil masterminds from taking over the world.

Every episode ended on a cliffhanger, with Harry strapped into an electric chair or locked in a safe underwater, about to be dropped into a tank of acid or even squashed by a falling elevator. The next episode would start with him escaping. *The Master Mystery* was so popular that Harry was asked to make a feature film . . .

THE GRIM GAME

The Grim Game was full of thrills. One scene had Harry dangling from a plane by a rope trying to get onto another plane—and of course, with no special effects in those days, all stunts had to be done for real. During filming, a freak wind made the two planes collide and they crashed to earth stuck together.

Luckily nobody was killed, so the film company released a photo of the tangled planes coming down and Harry told everyone he was lucky to be alive. **Nobody had seen a plane crash before**, so it was amazing publicity for the film, especially when Harry offered $1,000 to anyone who could prove the picture was faked. Of course, the crash was real, but what Harry didn't admit was that **he'd been on the ground at the time**—a stuntman had taken his place!

The Grim Game did so well that Harry started to spend a lot of time in Hollywood, and he made friends with the other big film stars of the time, including Charlie Chaplin. He liked being filmed because he only had to do a dangerous escape once and then it could be shown lots of times without him having to keep risking his life. There was also something else about it that Harry liked even better . . .

His next film, *Terror Island*, involved rescuing a girl from some terrifying natives, but this one had an unfortunate problem. The audiences thought the natives were hilarious and they **laughed in all the serious bits**, which left Harry as the daring hero looking rather silly!

Harry decided the only way to produce better films was to set up the Houdini Picture Corporation. He went on to make *The Man from Beyond* and *Haldane of the Secret Service*, but his films started to look a bit too similar—everybody knew that Harry would escape every time. His live shows were more exciting, because there was always the chance something would go wrong. In the end, Harry lost a lot of money, and in 1923 he gave up movies for good.

12   HARRY AND THE SPIRITS

Harry was fascinated by films and planes and all the other exciting new inventions that the world had to offer, but after his beloved mother died he became more and more involved with an idea that's been around since the time of the cavemen. He longed for a **message from the dead**.

He wasn't the only one. In the 1920s talking to the spirits was very fashionable. Over 100,000 Americans had died in the Great War, over 500,000 more were killed by a dreadful virus called Spanish Flu. **Thousands of people** wanted to contact their dead friends and relatives, and they were prepared to pay good money for it. Unfortunately, a lot of tricksters took advantage of this.

Harry and Bess had only ever pretended to talk to the dead in their spirit medium act in the medicine shows, but they both wondered whether some people had the power to do it for real. Of course Harry knew all the tricks that could be used to fool people, and the harder he looked to find a real medium, the more **crooks and fakes** he uncovered!

Mediums usually claimed to contact the dead by holding a séance, which would take place in a very dark room with everybody sitting around a table, fingertips touching. Often, the medium would have a

false hand on the table, while their real hand would be hidden in a black velvet glove so it could move objects around mysteriously. The medium might also have an assistant dressed head to toe in black velvet, who could make strange noises, cause things to fly around the room, and whisper into pipes to make creepy sound effects.

The medium might even use trick photographs showing, say, a **see-through head** hovering over a coffin. Photography was new in those days, and the pictures seemed a total mystery.

SIR ARTHUR

The search for a genuine medium was a tough one, but Harry had a very eager friend who kept him going.

Sir Arthur Conan Doyle wrote the Sherlock Holmes books, and at that time he was one of the world's **most famous** authors. Sir Arthur believed in spirits completely because his wife Jean was a well-known medium, and she had convinced him many times that she'd had messages from his relatives who had died in the war. Sir Arthur didn't care what other people told him—he even believed the ghostly photos! And when he suggested that spirits had helped Harry to break out of prisons and walk through walls, they ended up arguing . . .

June 16, 1922, Atlantic City, New Jersey

Harry and Sir Arthur were still great friends, however, and Jean did seem to have real powers. She didn't do silly tricks, and she didn't pretend to conjure up spirits whenever she wanted, so Harry was very excited one afternoon when Jean sent him a message. It was nine years after he'd lost his mom, and she was suggesting they hold a private séance.

When Harry arrived, Jean gave him a reassuring hug and they all sat down together. The room was bright and there was no sign of any trickery. Harry took the séance very seriously.

They closed their eyes and waited quietly for a few moments, then Jean snatched up a pencil and started to write **pages and pages and pages**. Sir Arthur passed the first sheet over. Harry's hand trembled as he read it.

The message went on and on until finally Jean finished and collapsed. Sir Arthur was thrilled. But Harry was sitting very quietly and seemed quite shocked. He was thinking about the date—June 16. **It was his mother's birthday** and they always celebrated, so why hadn't she mentioned it?

What's more, if this was a message from Cecilia, why was it in English? She always spoke in German! It also turned out that Jean had been asking Bess lots of questions about Cecilia before the séance.

Harry didn't want to upset Sir Arthur by suggesting Jean was a fake, but it all came out months later. The two friends **fell out completely**, especially when Harry challenged one of the people that Sir Arthur admired the most . . .

THE WITCH OF LIME STREET

In 1924 Harry started working with a panel of top scientists who offered $2,500 to anyone who could prove they could contact "the other side." All sorts of spirit mediums tried to win the money, and Harry made it his mission to **trap and expose** every one of them. He wasn't just out to make trouble—if ever he'd found a real spirit medium he would have been overjoyed.

Eventually all the mediums failed except one known as Margery. Her real name was Mina Crandon, but anyone who didn't believe in her called her the Witch of Lime Street. The experts, however, were totally convinced by her powers and were all set to award Margery the $2,500 prize money until Harry heard about it.

July 23, 1924, Boston, Massachusetts

Harry went with some of the experts to a séance at Margery's house, where he hoped to expose her. They all sat at the table holding hands, and Margery summoned her dead brother, Walter, into the room. His

voice boomed out from a megaphone on the table. Bells rang, objects flew off shelves, and at one point the megaphone hurtled straight toward Harry.

When the team left, Harry was deep in thought. He knew

how Margery did all but one of her tricks: he couldn't work out how she made the megaphone fly. He had known where both her hands were, and there was nobody else creeping around the room. **Then suddenly he realized**! When they were in the dark, there had been a moment when Margery had let go of his hand to cover her mouth as she did a little cough. She must have quickly put the megaphone on her head, before taking his hand again. She'd waited for a suitable moment, then flicked her head, throwing the megaphone at him.

Harry smiled at the others. "I've got her!" he said.

The team went back for one more séance. This time **the table rose right up** in the air and Harry caught Margery red-handed. She was bent over, lifting it up with her head! Nobody had ever suspected that before because it was such a weird thing to do! Even Harry had to admit . . .

It was the slickest ruse I ever detected!

THE VOICE OF DOOM

In the end Margery didn't get the prize, but oddly enough it was Margery's dead brother, Walter, who had the last word. During one of Margery's séances in August 1926, his voice said . . .

Houdini will be gone by Halloween . . .

HERE COMES THE SAD BIT

Harry was fifty-two years old, and he was still filling every second of every day doing big shows, flying planes, writing letters, running, swimming, and being president of the Society of American Magicians. Plus he was still as hungry as ever for new tricks, new places to visit, the latest inventions . . .

Two months after Walter's strange announcement, Harry was lying on the couch in his dressing room at the Princess Theater, in Montreal, Canada. Ten days earlier he had fractured his ankle doing the Chinese Water Torture Cell escape and it was still extremely painful, so he was resting it, getting ready for that night's show.

Harry had always kept up his boxing training, and one of his party tricks was to challenge people to **punch his stomach as hard as they could**. Some students were visiting his dressing room and one insisted on having a go. Harry was too proud to refuse. Though usually he would prepare himself by standing up and tensing his muscles, because of his ankle, he stayed flat on the couch and, before he had time to brace himself properly, the student **slammed his fist hard into Harry's stomach** again and again. The couch stopped Harry recoiling, which doubled the force of the punches.

Harry indicated for him to stop, then rolled aside. His stomach was hurting far more than he expected, but he went on and did his show that night and even had a party afterwards.

The next day Harry was in agony, from his ankle and his stomach, but he was so used to pain that he kept on working. What no one knew at the time was that Harry's appendix had been swollen for a few days, so the punches had done some very serious damage. Two days later he was six hundred miles away at the Garrick Theater in Detroit, and he felt even worse. He collapsed after his evening show and was rushed to the hospital. But the operation came too late.

Harry died a week later, on October 31, 1926. Halloween.

HELLO, HARRY?

Bess wasn't ready to let Harry go.

Despite all the frauds and fakes that Harry had exposed, they both still hoped there really was a spirit world, and in case one of them died **they had agreed a secret code**. If Bess got the right message from Harry, she would know that he was talking to her from the other side!

Bess always kept a photo of Harry with a candle burning beside it. She spoke to the photo every single day, and every year at Halloween, she held a séance, hoping for a reply. She would invite a good medium or friends she could trust to help, but she never heard the words she hoped for.

In 1936, Bess finally blew out the candle.

The Legend Lives On!

Harry had made sure that **his magic survived** after his death. He left all his equipment and the rights to perform his greatest tricks to Dash. It was a wonderful present and nobody deserved it more. Dash went out touring and was able to keep Harry's name on theater posters for another twenty years!

Find the squeeze a bit HARD-een?

You can't put a lid on Houdini.

Today there are hundreds of Houdini tribute acts who re-create the Chinese Water Torture Cell among other tricks. There are several Houdini museums, and an army of fans who collect Harry's books and posters and hunt through old bookshops for some of the thousands of letters he wrote. Devoted followers still hold séances trying to contact him!

Above all, Harry inspired generations of magicians and illusionists all over the world. Every single one of them owes a small part of their success to the man who started out in his mom's red woollen stockings as little "Ehrich, Prince of the Air" and went on to dazzle the world as the greatest showman of them all—Harry Houdini!

Thank you and goodnight.

TIMELINE

March 24, 1874:
Harry is born Ehrich Weisz
in Budapest, Hungary.

1878:
The Weisz family move to
America to join Harry's dad.

1875

1880

July 22, 1894:
Harry marries Bess Rahner.

1895:
Harry and Bess perform
together in New York City
and go on tour with the
Welsh Brothers Circus.

●1897:
"Dr. Hill's Medicine Show" comes to town. Harry performs as spirit medium, "Professor Houdini."

●1898:
Harry and Bess move into Harry's mother Cecilia's house. Harry sets up Professor Houdini's Magic School, but it fails.

1895

1900

●1899:
Harry performs in Minnesota and meets Martin Beck, who offers him a season of shows in one of his theaters.

Harry earns the name the "Handcuff King" for escaping handcuffs without a key.

●1900:
Harry and Bess leave on a European tour, starting in London.

1901:
Harry takes his mother to Budapest and throws her a lavish party.

1903:
Harry escapes a Siberian transport truck in Moscow.

1900

1904:
In London, Harry escapes from the "impossible" Mirror Handcuffs.

Harry buys his family a big house in New York.

September 20, 1905:
Harry challenges an imitator, Jacques Boudini, to jump into the Hudson River in shackles and escape.

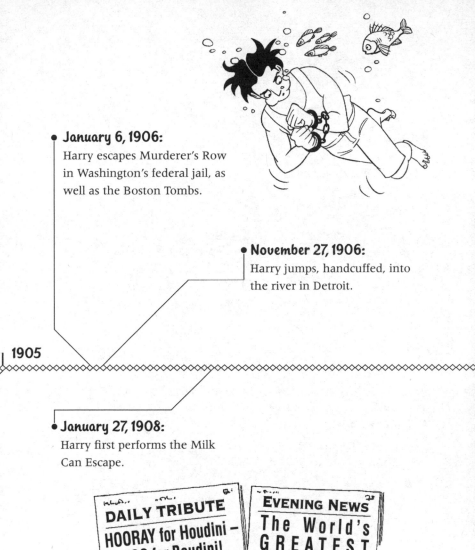

January 6, 1906:
Harry escapes Murderer's Row in Washington's federal jail, as well as the Boston Tombs.

November 27, 1906:
Harry jumps, handcuffed, into the river in Detroit.

1905

January 27, 1908:
Harry first performs the Milk Can Escape.

DAILY TRIBUTE
HOORAY for Houdini – BOO for Boudini!

EVENING NEWS
The World's GREATEST Showman Returns!

DAILY TIMES
Thousands watch the deadly river escape!

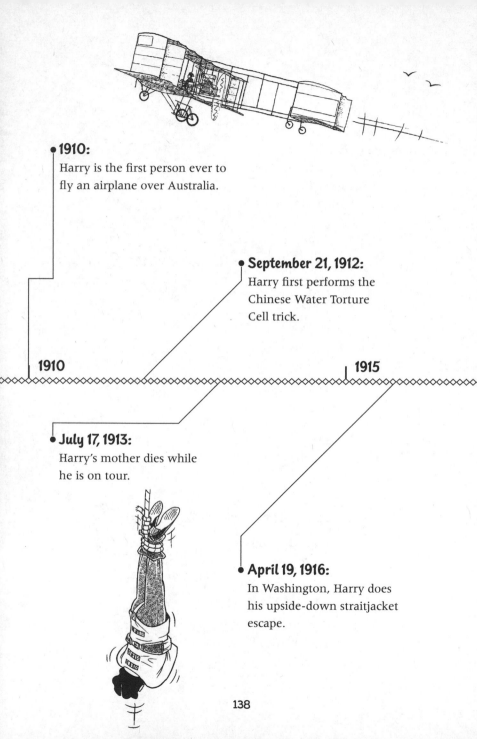

1910:
Harry is the first person ever to
fly an airplane over Australia.

September 21, 1912:
Harry first performs the
Chinese Water Torture
Cell trick.

1910   1915

July 17, 1913:
Harry's mother dies while
he is on tour.

April 19, 1916:
In Washington, Harry does
his upside-down straitjacket
escape.

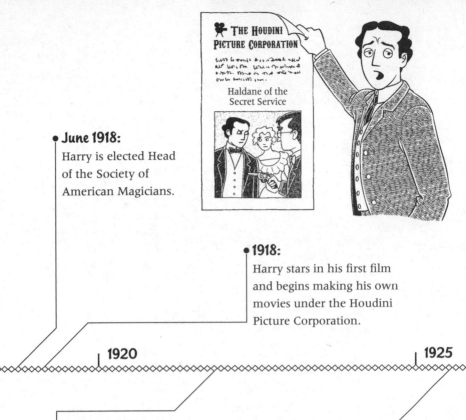

• June 1918:
Harry is elected Head
of the Society of
American Magicians.

THE HOUDINI
PICTURE CORPORATION

Haldane of the
Secret Service

• 1918:
Harry stars in his first film
and begins making his own
movies under the Houdini
Picture Corporation.

1920   1925

• June 16, 1922:
Sir Arthur Conan Doyle's
wife invites Harry to a séance
to try to make contact with
his mother.

• October 31, 1926:
Harry dies on Halloween.

GLOSSARY

Alhambra: The first London theater to book Harry as a performer.

appendicitis: A serious condition where the appendix becomes inflamed.

appendix: A small sac attached to the large intestine. Its purpose is not known.

asylum: A historic institution to treat people suffering from mental illness.

buttonhook: A hook with a handle for fastening buttons. Harry used these to pick locks.

Conan Doyle, Arthur: The author and creator of the Sherlock Holmes detective series.

Coney Island: A seaside amusement park in New York where Harry met Bess.

conjure: To cause something to appear.

contortionist: Someone who can bend their body in unusual ways.

Dime Museums: "Freak shows" that cost a dime to enter.

duel: A prearranged contest with deadly weapons between two people in order to settle a point of honor.

electromagnets: A piece of soft metal surrounded by a wire coil. When current passes through the coil, the metal becomes magnetic.

foreman: A worker who supervises and directs other workers.

gallows: A structure built to hang criminals.

handcuffs: A pair of metal rings which can be locked around a prisoner's wrists to prevent escape.

Hindu: A person who follows the religion Hinduism, which originated in Southeast Asia.

imposter: A person who pretends to be someone else in order to deceive others.

locksmith: Someone who makes and mends locks.

medium: A person who claims they can talk to the dead and pass their messages to the living.

metamorphosis: A complete change or transformation, such as in the life cycle of a butterfly.

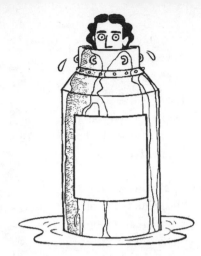

milk can: A galvanized steel can with a tight-fitting lid, used for shipping milk on a train.

patent: Gives someone the right to stop others from using or selling their invention.

rabbi: A Jewish scholar or teacher, especially one who studies or teaches Jewish law.

séance: A meeting where people try and contact the dead with the help of a medium.

Society of American Magicians: The oldest magic organization in the world.

Spanish Flu: An influenza outbreak during 1918. It was the deadliest virus in history.

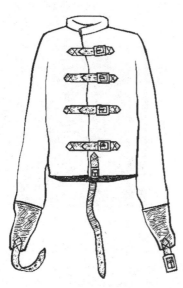

straitjacket: A belted jacket with sleeves buckled around the back that was used to restrain asylum patients during the late nineteenth and early twentieth centuries.

telegram: A written message sent using an electric device. The message was carried along wires in a code, and then the text was written or printed and delivered by hand or teleprinter.

SELECT BIBLIOGRAPHY

American Hauntings Ink. "The Haunted Museum: A Magician Among the Spirits." See www.americanhauntingsink.com/houdini.

Cox, John. Wild About Harry. See www.wildabouthoudini.com.

Encyclopedia of World Biography. "Harry Houdini Biography." See www.notablebiographies.com/Ho-Jo/Houdini-Harry.html.

The Great Harry Houdini (website). See www.thegreatharryhoudini.com.

Higbee, Joan F. "Houdini: A Biographical Chronology." American Memory Library of Congress; see memory.loc.gov/ammem/vshtml/vshchrn.html.

Kalush, William and Larry Sloman. *The Secret Life of Houdini: The Making of America's First Superhero*. New York: Atria Books, 2006.

Randl, James. *Houdini: His Life and His Art*. New York: Grosset & Dunlap, 1976.

Saltman, David. The Houdini File (website). See www.houdinifile.com.

Secrets to Magic Tricks, "Harry Houdini" (website). See secretstomagictricks.com/Articles/Harry%20Houdini.html.

Silverman, Kenneth. *Houdini!!! The Career of Ehrich Weiss*. New York: Perennial, 1996.

Taylor, Troy. "A Haunted Friendship: Houdini & Sir Arthur Conan Doyle." The Haunted Museum (website); see www.prairieghosts.com/doyle_houdini.html.

INDEX

Page numbers in *italics* refer to illustrations.

About the Author

Kjartan Poskitt is an award-winning author who has written more than eighty children's books. He lives in York, England, with his wife, four daughters, and a whole array of musical instruments.

About the Illustrator

Geraint Ford is an illustrator who has worked on everything from magazines to comics to children's books. He lives in England.

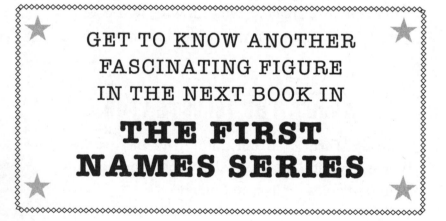

GET TO KNOW ANOTHER
FASCINATING FIGURE
IN THE NEXT BOOK IN

THE FIRST
NAMES SERIES

"For me, it was love at first flight!"

Andrew Prentice ★ Illustrated by Mike Smith

Introduction
Kansas, Winter 1907

It hadn't been this cold since eighteen-hundred-and-froze-to-death, but that didn't stop Amelia. She crouched over her sled and went through her pre-jump routine. Check the runners were free of ice. Check the snow was good. Check there weren't no lollygagging slowpokes clogging up her run.

Check. Check. Check.

"Here we go!" Amelia jumped, landed hard on her belly and shot down the hill like a comet.

When it snowed—and in Kansas, snow meant deep, glorious, school-obliterating blizzards—all the children in town knew there was only one place to be. The hill that ran from the top of North Second Street was perfect for sledding.

Traditionally, only the boys "belly-slammed." This meant they rode down the hill on their stomachs, head first. All the girls sat upright for a more ladylike trip.

Except for Amelia. She **loved speed more than anything** and didn't care what anyone thought. Amelia had always been different—and she **never got scared**.

A cart pootled out into the middle of the road. The hill was so icy that Amelia couldn't turn or stop. And she was going much too fast anyway. The horse had enormous blinkers, so it couldn't see her coming. The driver couldn't hear everyone's screams of warning. Amelia had about **three seconds to save her own life**. Plunging toward certain death, Amelia didn't blink. Instead she went faster, steering with her toes as she aimed for the only gap she could see.

Whoosh! Her sled zipped between the front and back legs of the horse so fast that the driver didn't even notice.

Soon, plenty of people *would* take notice of Amelia Earhart. In fact within thirty years she'd become the **most famous woman in the world**. She was bigger than the biggest movie stars. Hotter than the sun itself.

Amelia, you see, moved on from sleds to planes. She became a pilot—and back then, in the great golden age of flying, pilots were the best of the best. They soared across the heavens like heroes from legends. Adventure, danger and death were never far away.

Amelia became the most famous pilot of them all. She broke records, crossed oceans and achieved things that no one—man or woman—had ever achieved before.

She stayed different—and she never got scared.

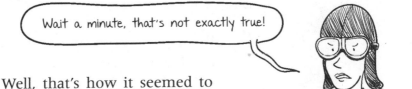

Wait a minute, that's not exactly true!

Well, that's how it seemed to everyone who knew you.

I got the jitters same as anyone, while I was getting ready. But they stopped as soon as I was up in the air. When you're flying, you're far too busy to be frightened.

So you worried when you were packing your suitcase?

Every time.

But when your instruments gave out, your engine was on fire, your plane was iced up and you started tumbling toward the hungry waves . . . **you weren't scared at all** then?

Not really. Thing is, when you're plummeting toward certain doom, you don't feel scared. You just "do". If you do right, you stay alive. And if you don't, well . . .

But why did you put yourself in all that danger, Amelia?

Well, if you'll just get on with my story you'll find out soon enough.

1   AMELIA ARRIVES

Amelia Mary Earhart zipped into the world on July 24, 1897. Her parents, Amy and Edwin Earhart, were delighted with their cheerful, fat little baby. They wrapped her up in blankets and nicknamed her Millie. A couple of years later they gave her a sister, Muriel. No one ever called her Muriel, though. The youngest Earhart was soon much better known as Pidge.

Millie's early years in Kansas and Iowa were happy ones. Her dad, Edwin, had a good job as a lawyer for the railways, though **he dreamed of bigger things**. In his spare time he tried to come up with an invention that would make his family's fortune. He squandered hundreds of dollars to make a new signal flag for trains, but sadly his flag never fluttered. As hard as Edwin tried, he never really got anywhere, which must have been frustrating.

There were some advantages to having a father who was a bit out of the ordinary. Take Christmas, for instance. Millie never wanted the girly presents she was expected to ask for. She wasn't interested in dolls, or pretty dresses; instead **she went for baseballs and fishing rods and sleds**. And her father gave them to her. He believed a girl should have what she wanted, no matter what anyone else said. And one Christmas,

Millie received a very unusual present.

It was a .22 caliber Hamilton rifle, to go with the packet of bullets she'd found in her stocking!

Not everyone was happy. Millie's grandparents were rich and they'd never approved of Edwin and his strange ways (they thought their daughter was too good for him). **Grandma almost fainted** with surprise.

Millie and Pidge had cleaned out the barn by the next morning.

Millie's dad wasn't just generous at Christmas. **He took his family on amazing adventures** as well.

The World's Fair was not really like any fair that Millie had visited or seen before. It was more like a gigantic, crazy, newly- built city, crammed with rides and shows and people from all over the world. You could go every day for a month and still never see the same thing twice.

You could visit the actual cabin where Abraham Lincoln was born; have your photo taken with Geronimo, the famous Apache war chief; or watch a real sea battle fought on the lake. You could ride double-dipping log chutes, visit a fake cloud that was someone's idea of what Heaven is actually like, and swoop about on **the greatest Ferris wheel ever built**.

Wow!

Even the food was mind-blowing. Some say the hot dog bun,

the cheeseburger, and the ice-cream cone were all invented at the fair.

When Millie came back home she was so excited about the rides that she made her uncle help her **build a roller coaster** in their back yard.

Millie was always good at planning, but even more importantly for someone with big dreams, she didn't just have ideas, she finished them off too. Her roller coaster was greased with lard and in their test runs without a rider it ran pretty fast.

Amelia insisted on being the first person to try it. She climbed up high, sat herself inside the crate, took a deep breath, and plunged.

It worked even better than she'd hoped. When she reached that little dip at the bottom, she didn't just coast to a stop, **she actually took off**, zooming through the air!

She came to rest meters away, covered in dust, cackling with laughter.

"Oh, Pidge!" Millie said. "It's just like flying. I'm going again."

This was too much for Millie's mom, who insisted that they take the coaster apart at once.

Dad's Sickness

In a way, that famous trip to the fair was too much for Edwin too. To fund the holiday, he'd squandered money they didn't have—just another bad decision in the series of bad decisions that he'd made and would keep on making. Soon, despite a promising career and a happy family, **Edwin started drinking** heavily.

Of course no one realized he had a problem, at first. To the children he was still their dad, as jolly and generous as ever. But the drinking was getting worse. He started making mistakes at work and hanging out in bars all afternoon. He broke promises and lied. He quarrelled with his wife.

Edwin's life spiralled quickly out of control and soon he was fired from his job. Millie and Pidge went away with their mom while he tried to sort himself out, but the family ran out of money and one winter **they couldn't even pay for firewood**.

"Dad's sickness" was awful for the girls. Not just because they lost their father, but because they'd lost their way of life too. Back then, the American Midwest was ruled by a strict moral code. You did the right thing. You went to church. You kept your head down and worked hard. You got married, and had children. You certainly didn't lose all your money and have a drunk for a father.

The Earharts were shamed and shunned. Suddenly Millie was an outcast. **She lost all her friends**. The family moved to a different town, but her father disgraced himself again, so she lost her new friends too. Fed up, Amy sent Edwin away again, and they moved to another house. Amelia ended up changing schools four times as a teenager.

> This hardened me up, I can tell you. I wouldn't wish it on anyone.

Those years must have been very tough. But Millie didn't react to her troubles the way you might think. Instead of trying to fit in and be like all the other girls in the new towns she moved to, she stubbornly insisted on doing things her own way.

Not Fair for Girls

Millie must have stuck out like a sore thumb. The other girls all wore skirts, but **Millie wore trousers** whenever she could—they felt more comfortable. She tried to play basketball with the boys. She complained that her teachers weren't teaching her properly. People always noticed how different she was, but she didn't care.

Look at her high school yearbook:

The thing was, Millie was always different.

2 AMELIA GETS A CHANCE

Amelia turned eighteen in 1915. She'd nearly grown up—she didn't call herself Millie anymore—and she had big dreams. She didn't want to just get married and have children, like most girls of the time. She wanted something else, though she wasn't quite sure what it was. But with no money and a disgraced family it was hard to see how she'd ever escape to a better world.

Then, out of the blue, **everything changed**. Amelia's upright, uptight granny died, and Amy Earhart inherited a bit of money. Suddenly she could afford to send Amelia and Muriel to a finishing school that would prepare them for college.

We needed a bit of a polish so we could pass our exams!

Amelia was over the moon—suddenly **a bigger and better world had opened up** for her just like that.

Even at her posh new school in Philadelphia, Amelia didn't change her ways, and by the end of her first year she'd managed to turn the place upside down. One story says she got the school's sorority system—a nasty, backstabbing popularity contest—banned. She campaigned to have modern subjects like science taught to the girls. She played the ukulele at midnight feasts. She was elected class vice president.

Keep the noise down— I've got exams tomorrow!

After years of struggle Amelia was flourishing; so it was a bit of a shock to everyone when she didn't finish her second year at the school.

Amelia's sister Muriel (hardly anyone called her Pidge anymore) was at a different school, in Toronto, and during the Christmas holidays Amelia went to visit her. In the Toronto train station, she was horrified when she noticed **four one-legged soldiers** helping each other down the platform. As soon as she left the station she saw there were many more terribly wounded soldiers—it was the first real evidence she'd seen of the World War I that was still raging in 1917. The soldiers' pain and sacrifice shocked Amelia and stirred something inside her.

Back at school her easy life seemed like a sideshow. Amelia knew **she had to do something**, anything, to help those soldiers. Before long she'd quit school forever.

I was nineteen and a grown woman. No one could stop me!

She sent a quick letter to her mother and jumped on the next train back to Canada. In Toronto she joined the Volunteer Aid Detachment (VAD) as a nurse and began caring for wounded and shell-shocked soldiers at the Spadina Military Hospital.

Amelia grew up fast. She worked long hours, six days a week. She scrubbed floors, ladled out medicine from a bucket, and played tennis with the soldiers. On her days off she went riding with her sister. Both of the Earhart girls were great with horses.

At the stables, one horse caught Amelia's eye: a notoriously bad-tempered stallion named Dynamite that no one had been able to ride.

The groom warned her that Dynamite had thrown two soldiers the day before. But **Amelia never backed down from a challenge**.

Read on in the next
FIRST NAMES book:
AMELIA EARHART

GET ON A FIRST NAME BASIS
WITH ALL THESE FAMOUS
FIGURES!

THE FIRST
NAMES SERIES

first names

HARRY Houdini

"Be with you in a minute!"

Kjartan Poskitt ★ Illustrated by Geraint Ford

first names

AMELIA Earhart

"For me, it was love at first flight!"

Andrew Prentice ★ Illustrated by Mike Smith

first names

ADA Lovelace

Beep!

"I dreamed up computer programming"

Ben Jeapes ★ Illustrated by Nick Ward

first names

MALALA Yousafzai

NOBEL PEACE PRIZE 2014

SCHOOL

NO GIRLS

"Don't tell me I can't go to school"

Lisa Williamson ★ Illustrated by Mike Smith